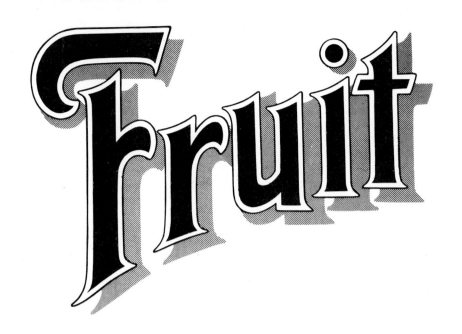

Fruit

Marshall Cavendish London & New York

Edited by Robin Wood

Published by Marshall Cavendish Books Limited
58 Old Compton Street
London W1V 5PA

© Marshall Cavendish Limited 1977, 1978, 1979

This material has previously appeared in the Marshall Cavendish
partwork *Grow Your Own*.

First printing 1979

Printed in Great Britain
by Henry Stone and Son Limited
Banbury

ISBN 0 85685 489 1

Introduction

Fresh fruit is no longer cheap to buy. It is expensive and likely to remain so. Yet given a little time and care—and the expert advice in this book—you can grow the popular tree and bush fruits we feature here. And, besides the considerable savings you will make, there is of course no better way of capturing the flavour and succulence of really fresh fruit than to pick it from your own garden.

Each chapter deals with a single crop, and gives you the detailed and comprehensive instructions you need to grow it to perfection. We begin with the basic facts about the crop—sowing to harvesting time, size and yield—to help you to plan your garden. Three types of symbols, explained below, are used to give an at-a-glance guide to the nature of the crop.

Then we give full details, with clear step-by-step illustrations, on preparing the soil, sowing the crop, caring for it during growth, harvesting and storing, and even preparing your prize products for exhibition.

Of particular value are the separate sections on identifying and combating the pests and diseases that threaten your products, as well as the guides to the most popular varieties available for your to choose from.

Practical both in size and format, *Fruit* will soon have earned its place on your gardening shelf.

low yield	minimum effort	crops in three months or less
medium yield	needs more care	crops in 4–12 months
high yield	requires special attention	crops in over 12 months

Contents

Fruit

Apples

Malus pumila (fam. *Rosaceae*)
Hardy deciduous tree, with a useful life of about
50 years.
Planting to harvesting time: dwarf trees on M9
rootstock produce fruit when about three years old. More
vigorous trees take a year or so longer.
Size: from about 1.8 m (6′) tall for dwarf bushes to about
7.5 m (25′) for standard trees. Up to 12 m (40′) for crab and
cider apples.
Yield: dwarf bush trees may average about 18 kg (40 lb) a
year; bush trees, 36 kg (80 lb), and mature cider apple trees
may yield 500 kg ($\frac{1}{2}$ ton).

The apple is probably the most widely grown tree fruit because it is reasonably hardy and there are varieties to suit most soil and weather conditions. Even a neglected apple tree will produce some kind of crop, but all too often the wormy or diseased fruit harvested from neglected trees could easily be avoided. With a little care, a mature tree can be restored to vigorous cropping within a couple of seasons and will supply the family with large supplies of delicious fruit.

Apples are a rewarding crop to grow in the small garden. It does not take long for a young tree to start fruiting; dwarfing rootstock can be chosen to restrict the size of the tree so that it will not outgrow its site; a small number of trees will provide all the apples that a family will want, and careful selection of varieties can ensure fruit almost all year round.

The trees will grow happily in most temperate regions. They need a sunny, well-drained site which is sheltered and frost-free at blossom time to ensure that insects can pollinate. They will not grow in gardens waterlogged for long periods, although there is a way of overcoming this problem (see over). Cooking apples are more tolerant than dessert ones of heavy clay soil, high rainfall and indifferent drainage—and they can survive with less sunshine.

Types of apple

Apples can be divided into four groups: cooking apples, dessert (or eating) apples, cider apples and crab apples. The last two groups can be planted as pollinators for the others.

Cookers are sharply flavoured and are not usually eaten raw. They tend to have a longer season, to keep better and are more tolerant of less-than-perfect conditions than dessert apples, but they do, however, need more nitrogenous fertilizer.

Sweeter in flavour, and mainly eaten raw, are the dessert apples. These are smaller than cooking apples and have a shorter eating season. The trees dislike

A modern dwarf bush apple tree — convenient to look after and ideal for the small gardener.

rainfall of more than 1 m (40″) a year.

Choosing trees

A combination of cooking and dessert apples suits most families best. Nearly all apple trees must have another variety nearby flowering at the same time, if they are to bear fruit, so you should plant a minimum of two. Most varieties have plenty of pollen and will pollinate one another, provided their flowering seasons coincide or overlap. Some have little pollen—they are known as triploid and need a suitable pollinator to set their fruit. Triploids will not pollinate the other tree, however, so in this case there should be a third variety present (not triploid) to ensure a good crop on all three.

A very few varieties are self-fertile but all will give bigger crops if pollinated by another.

Tree shapes: the simplest and most appropriate form of tree for the small garden is the bush. These small, free standing trees are simple to manage and the fruit can be easily harvested. For very small sites they can be obtained in dwarf forms needing as little as 1.5 m (5′) space.

Apple trees can, however, be trained in several different shapes, some of which are particularly useful. Cordons are excellent space savers grown on walls or fences, or can be used in a row as a screen. Fans are also suitable for a large wall, but apple trees should not be placed in too warm a site. The espalier, with branches trained at regular intervals at right angles from the trunk, and dwarf pyramid trees are also popular.

If you want to train a tree into one of these artificial shapes, you must buy a maiden—a one-year-old. The inexperienced gardener may find it easier to buy a ready trained tree, two or three years old, from the nurseryman. Maintaining the shape is then relatively simple. Training cordon trees is described in this chapter.

3

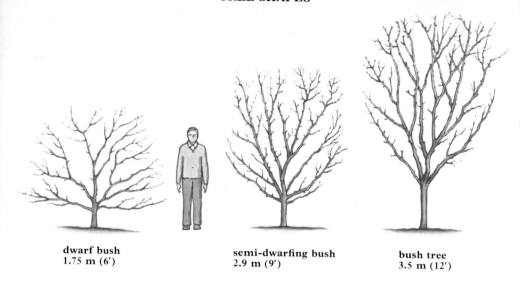

dwarf bush
1.75 m (6′)

semi-dwarfing bush
2.9 m (9′)

bush tree
3.5 m (12′)

Rootstocks: nowadays trees are formed by joining the apple variety to a separate root system or 'stock'. The fruiting habit of the resulting tree is that of the top, called the scion, but the size is determined by the rootstock.

The development of what are called dwarfing rootstocks means that now small trees are available which fruit abundantly. The research was carried out at East Malling Research Station and at Merton in England and their rootstocks, referred to as M (Malling) and MM (Malling Merton), are used throughout the world. By choosing between rootstocks you can select the variety you want at the size you want. For instance, M9 rootstock produces the most dwarf trees, M26 more vigorous ones and MM106 and M7 semi-dwarf specimens. If you are buying a tree, the nursery catalogue will explain the differences in detail.

There are trees available with several varieties (usually three) grafted on to the same roots. These 'family trees' are particularly suitable where space is very limited. The three varieties will pollinate each other and you will have a selection of types of apple.

Age of tree: if you intend to train an apple on a fence or wall yourself, buy a maiden (one-year-old tree). You will, however, get fruit sooner by buying a two or three-year-old cordon or bush. But do not let trees bear more than one or two sample fruit each in their first summer—give the roots time to re-establish.

Preparing the soil

A medium loam, slightly acid and well-drained, is the perfect type of soil.

If possible, prepare the soil in summer by deep digging to improve surface drainage and get rid of perennial weeds. If you cannot prepare the soil so far in advance, firm the ground well by treading or rolling it after digging. Then leave it to settle for two weeks or more before planting.

If the soil is very acid make it less so by applying lime. Improve a neutral or only just alkaline soil by working in manure and use acid fertilizers such as sulphate of ammonia when necessary. The lack of nutrients caused by highly alkaline soil can be corrected by modern artificial fertilizers and foliar sprays.

Work in liberal quantities of manure, garden compost, peat or leafmould to improve the consistency of both light, sandy or gravelly soil, and do the same

PLANTING A TREE

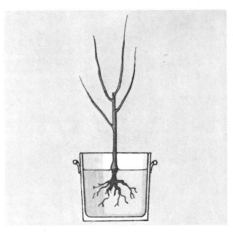

1. If roots have dried out, soak in water for about an hour.

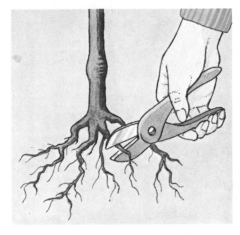

2. Trim back damaged roots. Make a slanting cut in thicker roots.

3. If planting is delayed, bury roots in a trench, up to soil mark on stem.

4. Place stick across hole to check planting depth. Soil mark on stem should align with the stick.

5. Drive in upright stakes 23 cm (9″) away from tree. Return soil, making sure it penetrates between the roots.

6. Tread the soil down firmly and level off. Make sure the union of rootstock and scion is above ground.

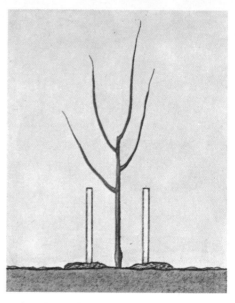

7. Apply surface mulch of rotted compost, manure or peat, but avoid touching the stem.

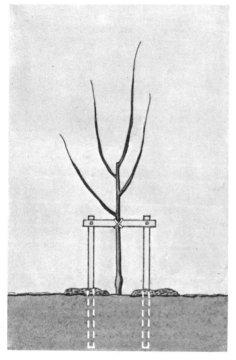

8. Erect a crosspiece between the stakes, to run below the bottom branch of the tree. Tie the tree to the crosspiece.

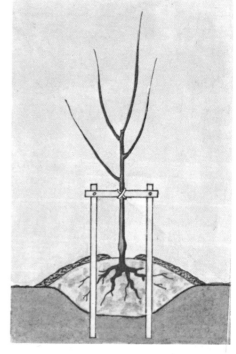

9. Planting method for badly drained ground: create a mound above a shallow hole to raise tree roots above the normal level.

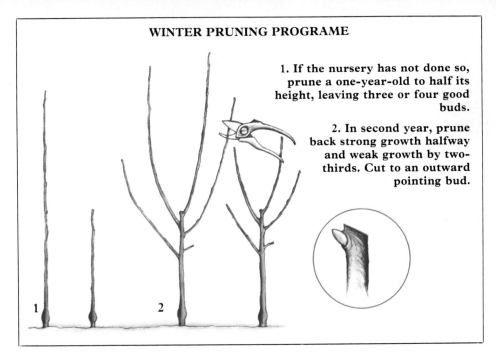

WINTER PRUNING PROGRAME

1. If the nursery has not done so, prune a one-year-old to half its height, leaving three or four good buds.

2. In second year, prune back strong growth halfway and weak growth by two-thirds. Cut to an outward pointing bud.

thing for heavy clay soils.

If you are planning to grow apples in a kitchen garden where there has been a high level of feeding, beware! Tree growth, especially of dessert apples, will be stimulated to the detriment of fruit blossom. Delay tree-planting for a year, meanwhile do not fertilize the ground but go on growing vegetables.

Planting

Planting is possible at any time during the dormant season–when there are no leaves on the tree–so long as the ground is neither frozen hard nor too wet to work freely. The soil should be crumbly, not pasty. Soon after leaf-fall is best.

Plant the trees as soon as they are delivered, if possible. If the roots have dried out in transit soak them in water in a dustbin for about an hour. Trim back any damaged roots, making slanting cuts on the underside of thicker roots.

If for any reason planting has to be delayed, heel trees in temporarily in the open. Make a trench, with one side sloping at an angle of about 45°, deep enough to bury the roots up to the soil

mark on the stem, which shows the depth to which the tree was growing in the nursery. Lay the tree in this trench and cover the roots with soil just up to the soil mark. Tread in lightly.

The trees should not be planted too close together. For bush trees on MM106 rootstock in average quality soil, allow a radius of 2 m (7') around each bush. In rich soil, increase this to 2.8 m (9'). Bushes on M26 rootstock need a radius of 1.75 m (6') space. For the smallest trees on M9 rootstock, allow a radius of 1.5 m (5') and for vigorous growers on dwarf M9 rootstock, 1.75 m (6'). Family trees need a spacing of at least 4.25 m (14').

Try to get someone to help you when you plant the trees. An extra pair of hands will make it much easier to position a tree straight and upright. Dig each planting hole wide and deep enough for all the roots to be spread out fully in their natural growing position. When you have finished planting and treading down the soil, the tree should be at exactly the same soil depth as it was when growing in the nursery. The join of the rootstock and the scion (called the union) must not be below ground level, or the scion may put out its own rootstock.

To check that your planting hole is of the right depth, lay a stick across it to show you the ground level and hold the tree in its planting position in the hole. The level of the stick should match the mark on the stem of the soil from its former planting.

All bush trees need staking. Use 5 cm (2″) diameter stakes which have been treated with a copper-based preservative. Drive two upright stakes into the planting hole, each about 23 cm (9″) away from the tree. In light soil they should eventually be buried 60 cm (2′) below soil level, in heavy soil 45 cm (1′ 6″).

Put a spadeful of soil into the bottom of the hole, spread out the roots, sprinkle over a few handfuls of moist peat and start returning the soil. If soil is rather poor, mix a couple of handfuls of sterilized bonemeal with the soil waiting to go back into the planting hole, but not in immediate contact with the roots. Get a helper to wriggle the tree a little so the soil filters well between the roots. Tread the soil down to firm it as you go.

Water with one 12 L (2½ gal) bucketful and, if there is no rain within a week, give it another bucketful.

Level off the soil and surround the tree as far as the branches extend with a surface mulch of well-rotted compost, manure, leafmould or damp peat, but do not let this touch the tree stem or it may rot the bark.

As soon as the tree is planted fix a crosspiece to the two stakes, a little below the lowest branch, and fasten the tree to it. Use a purpose-made plastic tree tie for this job, or wrap a piece of sacking or cloth around the tree to protect the bark and tie over it with soft string. Finish by twisting the string between the tree and stake to prevent chaffing.

During the early months the soil will settle and the tie may need repositioning.

THINNING FRUITLETS

Thin dessert apples to improve size and appearance of fruit. Use a thin pointed pair of scissors and cut out the central fruitlet in each cluster and then any diseased or smaller fruitlets. Leave only one or two fruit on each cluster.

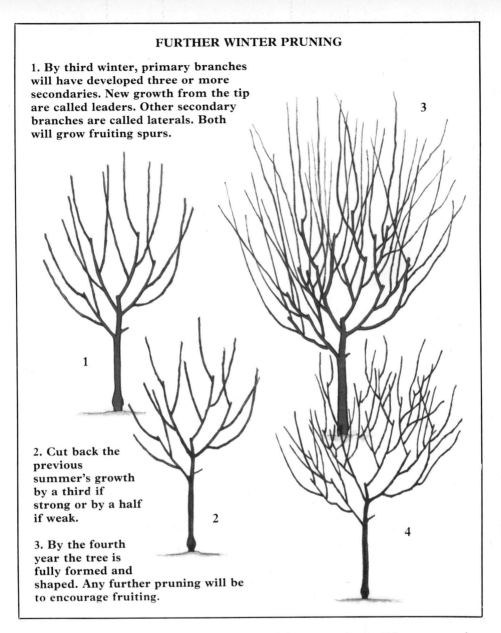

FURTHER WINTER PRUNING

1. By third winter, primary branches will have developed three or more secondaries. New growth from the tip are called leaders. Other secondary branches are called laterals. Both will grow fruiting spurs.

1

3

2. Cut back the previous summer's growth by a third if strong or by a half if weak.

2

4

3. By the fourth year the tree is fully formed and shaped. Any further pruning will be to encourage fruiting.

In two or three years the tree may be able to dispense with support.

Planting on badly drained land
If you want to grow dessert apples and the ground is badly drained, you can plant on a slight mound.

Make only a shallow depression instead of digging a deep planting hole. Stand the tree in this, insert its stakes and then mound up soil from some other part of the garden to the soil mark on the stem. The mound must be wider than the existing extent of the roots to encourage them to grow outwards. Mulching extends further than the branches and therefore each year you will have to topdress further out.

This method can be used also where shallow top soil overlies chalk at a depth

PLANTING AND SUMMER PRUNING OF CORDONS

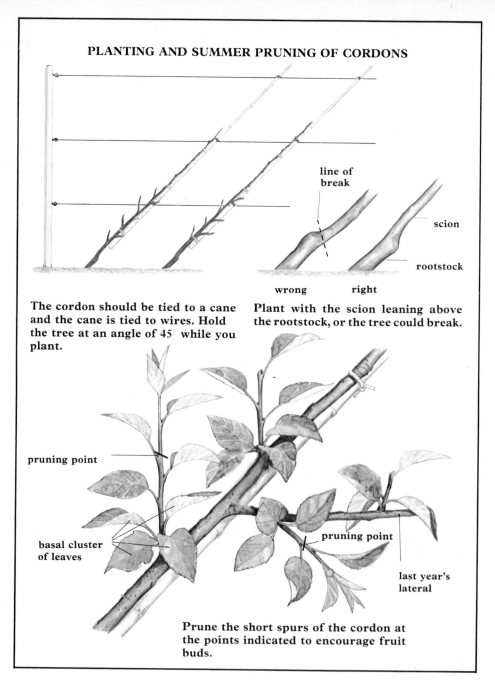

line of break

scion

rootstock

wrong   right

The cordon should be tied to a cane and the cane is tied to wires. Hold the tree at an angle of 45 while you plant.

Plant with the scion leaning above the rootstock, or the tree could break.

pruning point

basal cluster of leaves

pruning point

last year's lateral

Prune the short spurs of the cordon at the points indicated to encourage fruit buds.

of about 45 cm (1′ 6″).

Trees grown on mounds are more vulnerable to drought, and plenty of watering is essential in dry periods, particularly in early life. A mulch of garden compost or leafmould to arrest surface evaporation is very important.

Watering and feeding

The first spring is a critical time for newly planted trees. In the first few summers it is essential to water freely and in adequate quantities, and a surface mulch will do much to conserve moisture in the soil.

Give no more manure in the first season. In succeeding winters, dress the ground around each tree a little further out then the branches extend. Use 38 g per sq m (1¼ oz per sq yd) of sulphate of ammonia and 22 g per sq m (3/4 oz per sq yd) of sulphate of potash. Rake the fertilizers into the surface in late winter.

Thereafter, every other year rake in, at the same time, 52 g per sq m (1 3/4 oz per sq yd) of superphosphate. If the harvest has been heavy, an extra fertilizer dressing is beneficial.

Pruning

Winter pruning is to build a framework of robust main branches. Standards, half-standards and bushes are pruned the same way.

Immediately after planting give the tree its first pruning with sharp secateurs. Hard winter pruning stimulates the wood growth necessary at this stage of the tree's development. If it is an unpruned maiden tree cut it back to half its height, leaving three or four good buds.

If you have bought a two-year-old tree, it will have only three or four branches. If these are strong and long, cut each back half way, making your cut close beyond a growth bud pointing outwards.

If these first branches are thin and wispy and not very long, be more drastic and cut off two-thirds of the length of each. This cutting back will cause growth buds near the cut ends to develop.

By the tree's third winter each of the primary branches will have made three or more secondary branches. Cut back the previous summer's growth by a third if strong, by a half if thin and wispy.

Some sideshoots (the laterals) may have grown from the secondary branches by now. If these laterals are badly placed to make new branches, cut each back to its fourth bud. Any sideshoots springing

from the trunk of the tree just below the main branches should be sliced off flush with the stem.

Four-year-old trees are regarded as adult. From now on winter pruning is restricted to the minimum necessary to ensure a continuing supply of fruiting wood, rather than to extend the size of the tree. Remove crossing branches and cankerous or broken ones.

If you do not prune a sideshoot, it will make fruit buds in its second year. These are bigger, fatter and rounder than growth buds and the next year will blossom in spring. Every winter leave at least some sideshoots unpruned to bear fruit. If more sideshoots are needed, cut back some to the second bud from the base. But, in general, cut back just the three-year-old sideshoots which have fruited to a 5 cm (2") stump.

Do not touch the tips of the branches once fruit-bearing has begun—unless a branch is growing in an undesirable direction and you want to replace the season's new extension growth (the leader) with another one. Some varieties also form fruit buds at the tips of one-year-old shoots. Leave such shoots intact.

This system of pruning will produce a balance of fruiting laterals and vegetating ones to provide fruit later on.

Training cordons

A cordon consists of a single stem bearing fruiting spurs. The tree is planted at an angle to restrict growth and to encourage early fruiting and an even production of buds. Three different varieties can be grown in one 3 m row.

Rows should run from south to north if at all possible. Put in 2.25 m (7′ 6″) sturdy posts, about 3 m (10′) apart. Stretch three 2.5 mm ($\frac{1}{10}$″) gauge galvanized wires between posts at heights of 60 cm (2′), 1.2 m (4′) and 1.8 m (6′). Use an adjustable fence strainer at the end of each wire to keep it taut. Fix a 2.4 m (8′) long bamboo cane to the wires at an angle of 45° where each tree is to be planted.

Plant two to three-year-old cordons 75 cm (2′ 6″) apart at an angle of 45° with the tip pointing away from the midday sun. Space rows 1.8 m (6′) apart.

About 10 cm (4″) from the soil mark there is a swelling where the scion is joined to the rootstock. This is the union. Hold the whole tree at an angle for planting with the scion uppermost on the rootstock. Planted the other way round the tree could break off its roots.

As soon as it is planted, the cordon must be tied to its supporting bamboo cane. Tie in three places—the lowest one 5 cm (2″) above the union.

Pruning cordons

Pruning is necessary in the first winter for tip-bearing types. With these, cut back just the main stem by a quarter of the previous season's growth. Repeat in subsequent winters.

The main pruning is done in mid-summer in warmer districts and up to a month later in cooler ones. Start when you see that sideshoots growing directly from the main cordon stem are maturing–when they are more than 23 cm (9″) long, the leaves have lost their early brightness and become a deep green and the skin of the shoot has stiffened and begun to look bark-like for the lower part of its length.

At the base of such shoots you will usually find a cluster of leaves. Ignore these, count three leaves from the base of the shoot and then cut close after the third leaf. There may also be growths springing from laterals made and pruned in a previous year. Cut each back to the first leaf beyond the basal cluster. If some new shoots are not mature, wait until they are before pruning. If secondary growth occurs in late summer from near the point where you made the first cuts, prune such shoots back to one leaf or bud in mid-autumn.

In about three years, when the cordon reaches the length of its cane, unfasten the cane from the wires and bend the whole tree down about 5 and refasten the cane. Repeat again in a few years

if it appears to be necessary.

Usually there comes a time when the mature tree stops producing further extension growth each summer. But if it reaches the limit of space before this happens, cut it back in spring soon after new growth begins.

Except in the case of tip-bearing varieties, the leader should not normally be pruned until it must be checked for lack of space. If the desired fruit-bearing sideshoots are scarce, however, stimulate the production of more by pruning the season's new extension growth of the leader by one third in winter. To encourage individual buds in a bare length of stem, cut a half-moon notch from the bark just above them.

If after some years there are too many fruiting spurs and they are getting crowded, in winter cut some back and take out others entirely.

Thinning out the fruit

If an apple tree bears a very heavy crop in any one year, it may take a rest the next season. The big crop, too, is likely to be of undersized fruit.

Dessert apples are thinned out to improve the appearance and size of the individual fruit. Cookers tend to be naturally larger and are not usually thinned. Fruit thinning is less likely to be required on dwarf trees growing on M9 rootstock and trees trained as cordons.

Some shedding of fruit occurs naturally about mid-summer or just after, but the earlier you do any thinning the better for the tree. As soon as the fruitlets have 'set' (when a tiny but obvious fruitlet has replaced the blossom and you know a heavy crop is possible) take a thin pointed pair of scissors and cut out the central fruitlet from each cluster. This 'king apple' often proves to be mis-shapen and of poor keeping quality. Remove any blemished fruitlets and continue thinning until only one or two fruit remain out of each cluster. These fruit should never be closer than 10 cm (4″) to the next cluster.

If the crop is heavy, support the branches with stakes.

Harvesting the crop
When you think an apple is ripe, lift it in the palm of your hand and give it the slightest possible twist. If it comes away easily, it is ready. Take care not to bruise the fruit. Cider and crab apples grown in grass may be allowed to drop off.

Apples intended for storing should be picked just before they are ripe or they will quickly deteriorate but care must be taken not to tear the shoots when picking an unripe crop. Cooking apples may be used before they are ripe but their full flavour will develop with keeping. Cider apples should mature on the tree. Do not leave late crops of dessert apples on the tree after the end of October.

Storing the crop
The ideal storage place for apples is one which is cool–just below 5°C (40°F) – well-ventilated, dark and slightly moist. A loft, garage or shed is usually too dry for this purpose, but by storing the fruit in plastic bags, this problem can be overcome.

Store only sound dry fruit and do not mix varieties in one bag. Use lots of small bags so that any rot cannot spread far. After sealing them snip off a finger-nail sized triangle from each bottom corner to ventilate.

Exhibition tips
Pick ripe perfect fruit and leave on the stalks—all fruit is shown with the stalks in place.

Select only fruit of the same colour, form and size.

Dessert apples should be no more than 7.5 cm (3″) across—about 7 cm (2¾″) is the most favoured size.

Wrap each apple separately in tissue paper and pack in a box of crumpled newspaper to take them to the show.

Stiff paper plates are favoured for displaying fruit. Apples are never polished for shows and usually only one variety is displayed on a plate.

Pests & Diseases
Apples can be attacked by a number of pests and diseases–some of the more common are described below. A regular spraying programme will keep many of them in check: scab, mildew, caterpillars eating leaves (winter moth etc) or fruitlets (sawfly), aphids of various kinds, capsids, apple suckers, red spider mite and scale insects. American blight (woolly aphids), codling moth, canker, brown rot and bitter pit, however, will not be controlled by the spray programme.

Birds may do much damage to buds in winter. A netting fruit cage may be practical for small trees, otherwise, swathe trees in the rayon web sold at garden shops for the purpose.

Every second or third year spray with a tar oil solution during the tree's dormant (leafless) period. This will control the eggs of aphids, winter moth and suckers, as well as adult scale insects. It will also clean the bark of lichen and moss which harbour troubles.

Spraying programme
Each year give the tree three spray treatments. The first is when the leaves are unfolding at 'green cluster' stage: captan to control scab, and malathion against aphids, capsids, apple suckers and winter moth caterpillars.

Donald Smith

Brown, ribbon-like scars indicate damage by the maggots of the apple sawfly.

The next spray, about two weeks later when the blossom buds are showing pink, contains captan and dinocap (for mildew).

The third spray is at petal fall when nearly all blossom is off. *Never spray fully opened flowers, because of the danger to bees and other pollinating insects.* This spray is against pests and diseases already mentioned, plus apple sawfly caterpillars.

Pesticides can usually be applied together, *but not all are compatible,* so follow the maker's instructions.

As an alternative to a regular programme of spraying you can spray only if trouble appears and cut out shoots affected by such diseases as mildew or by pests like leaf-curl aphid. Regular feeding of course will do much to aid the tree's resistance to fungal diseases and natural predators may help to keep down pests.

Aphids: these widespread pests cause young leaves and shoot tips to curl. Leaves become sticky and sooty-looking. The insects are small, green or grey in colour, and live on the underside of leaves. Remove and destroy aphids as soon as they appear and spray with an insecticide, for example, malathion.

Apple sawfly: the white maggots of apple sawfly eat into the side of fruitlets leaving a sticky mess at the entrance. The resulting apples bear ribbon-like scars. Spray with malathion when most of the flower petals have fallen.

Apple sucker: attack by this pest shows itself as waxy threads on the flower trusses leading to brown discoloration of petals and a failure to unfold. It feeds on the sap in the same way as aphids and is controlled by the same insecticides: tar oil in winter, or malathion in spring.

Capsid: damage is mainly in the fruitlets, which develop pale scabs and become distorted in shape. Leaves are punctured, puckered and tattered. Control as for aphids.

Codling moth: the grubs of the codling moth have a brown head. From mid-summer they enter the fruit near the eye and eat the centre. Affected fruit becomes highly coloured and drops early. Spray with fenitrothion four weeks after petals fall and again three weeks later. To avoid this pest, tie a band of sacking round the trunk in early mid-summer in which the caterpillars will pupate. Remove and burn band and cocoons in winter.

American blight (woolly aphid): as the name suggests, this pest is covered with white fluff. It commonly feeds on

Ministry of Agriculture Food and Fisheries

Murphy Chemicals

An infestation of the white fluff-covered woolly aphid, also known as American blight.

Symptoms of canker on a branch, showing shrunken, flaking bark.

the junctions of branches resulting in warty growths; the bark cracks, which allows the entry of canker and other fungal diseases. Malathion sprayed in early summer, repeated two weeks later, or brushing with methylated spirits, will control the aphids.

Red spider mite

These minute pale red insects live on the undersides of leaves and are particularly active in hot dry summers. The leaves become a speckled, dull, pale yellow or grey green, wither and fall early, and new growth is stunted. Spray with derris or malathion.

Scab: this fungus disease produces black or brown spots on leaves and fruit, which later cracks and may become infected with brown rot. It is worst in a wet spring and is treated with captan. Spray at bud-bursting stage and repeat twice at 14-day intervals.

Canker: the most common fungus disease of the wood of branches, trunk and shoots, canker is especially active where soil is badly drained. The bark becomes sunken, and flakes and dies where fungus enters through tree wounds. If it encircles the stem, the branch above will die. Wherever flaking bark is seen, cut back the wood below the infection to healthy growth, making a

ICI Agricultural Division, Millbank

The effects of brown rot on fruit—the brown fruit often remains 'mummified' on the tree.

clean cut just above a joint. Burn infected wood. Treat any large wound with a fungicidal paint.

Mildew: white powdery patches on leaves and young shoots in spring, and infected flowers which turn cream in colour and do not set, are produced by mildew. Remove infected shoots and spray with dinocap.

Bitter pit: bitter pit causes small brown pits in the flesh, giving it a bitter taste. Spray the leaves with calcium nitrate at two to three-week intervals from early to late summer. Less hard pruning, less nitrogenous fertilizer and regular watering will keep it in check.

Brown rot: this disease infects the fruit, which turns brown then either drops, or remains mummified on the tree to infect next year's fruit. Fruit with brown skin or flesh should be destroyed as soon as seen—not stored.

GUIDE TO APPLE TROUBLES

Symptoms	Probable Causes
Holes in fruitlets with sticky mess around them	Apple sawfly
Discoloured petals on partly opened bossom buds	Apple suckers
Misshapen fruitlets	Capsid
Curling leaves and shoot tips	Aphids
Hole at eye end of fruit	Codling moth
Soft warty growth on bark	American blight
Speckled leaves	Red spider mite
Sunken, flaking bark	Canker
White powdery patches on leaves	Mildew
Brown pitting in apple flesh	Bitter pit
Fruit turning brown	Brown rot
Black or brown spots on fruit and leaves	Scab

15

Varieties

To set a crop, most apples need to be cross-pollinated. Most varieties have plenty of pollen and will pollinate one another, *provided their flowering seasons coincide, or overlap.* Some have little pollen—they are known as triploid. They need a suitable pollinator to help them set their fruit, but they themselves will not pollinate the other tree. In this case there should be a third variety present (not triploid) to ensure a good crop on all three. A few varieties are self-fertile though they crop better with a suitable pollinator.

As previously mentioned there are literally hundreds of different varieties of apple. Below are some of the more readily available dessert and cooking apples, and some crab apples.

Varieties of dessert apple

Beauty of Bath: small apple; heavily striped bright red; crops prolifically; ready late mid-summer; not advisable for planting in frosty gardens; does not store, slightly tip-bearing; *flowers early.*

Egremont Russet: medium; yellow, heavily covered in brown russet; crisp and well-flavoured; suitable for the small garden—makes good cordons; ready mid-autumn to early winter; heavy cropper and disease-resistant; *flowers early.*

James Grieve: medium to large; yellow, striped and flushed red; good cropper; ready early autumn; tends to canker on heavy soil; *flowers mid-season.*

Coxes Orange Pippin: medium yellow-orange with red flush and stripes; crisp with superb flavour; ready mid-autumn, stores to late mid-winter; crop moderate to heavy; spurs well but not advisable in wet areas; *flowers mid-season; proven best pollinator James Grieve.*

Winston: medium; green, covered in stripes and flush of dull red; good flavour, slightly sharp; ready mid-winter, stores until mid-spring; crop moderate to light; good as cordon; *flowers mid-season, self-fertile.*

Tydeman's Early Worcester: medium, pale green heavily flushed with red; crops well; ready late summer; slightly tip-bearing; *flowers early to mid-season.*

Fortune: medium; yellow with long red stripes and flushed red; crisp, good flavour; ready early to mid-autumn; crop moderate; *flowers mid-season.*

George Cave: bright yellow and red good regular cropper; juicy and crisp, slightly acid; *flowers early.*

Laxton's Epicure: yellow-green, flushed and streaked with red; sweet and juicy, best eaten as soon as picked; heavy cropper; *flowers mid-season.*

Ashmead's Kernel: greenish-yellow russet; firm with first-class flavour; moderate cropper; *flowers mid-season.*

Beauty of Bath

Egremont Russet

Orleans Reinetter: yellow-gold, blotched with russet; juicy and well-flavoured; heavy cropper; *flowers late.*

Discovery: medium-sizes greenish yellow fruit flushed with scarlet; crops early autumn; *flowers mid-season.*

Varieties of cooking apple

Bramley's Seedling: large; green but flushed red in the crimson-skinned sort; excellent flavour and cooks very well; ready late autumn and stores until mid-spring; crop mostly heavy, but makes large tree and not suitable for small gardens; *flowers mid-season; N.B. triploid variety.*

Grenadier: medium to large; yellow-green apple; very good flavour; ready late summer to mid-autumn; crop heavy and regular; good for small gardens; not prone to disease; *flowers mid-season; self-fertile.*

Peasgood Nonsuch: large; golden-yellow, flush bright crimson, good as baking apple; crop moderate, needs deep well-drained loam; good for small gardens; *flowers mid-season.*

Lane's Prince Albert: greenish-yellow, streaked red; juicy white flesh; good cropper; suitable for small gardens; *flowers mid-season (flowers for a long time).*

Edward VII: medium; yellow when fully ripe; good cooker (and dessert if kept); keeps very well; *flowers very late*

(a 'wise apple' which often escapes late frosts).

Rev. W. Wilks: very large; yellow, striped with scarlet; good exhibition fruit; excellent for baking; rather acid; does not keep long; heavy cropper; *flowers early; self-fertile, (and not a good pollinator as it flowers irregularly).*

Howgate Wonder: large; green, striped red; good tree for the smaller garden; cooks well; heavy cropper; *flowers mid-season.*

Varieties of crab apple

Dartmouth: small; deep red fruit; ready mid-autumn; good for jelly making; forms a spreading head; *flowers mid-season.*

John Downie: small; conical shape; yellow, flushed bright red; ready early autumn; good for preserves; upright head; *flowers mid-season.*

Golden Hornet: bright yellow fruits the size of cherries; stiff erect habit; fruits suitable for jelly-making; *flowers mid-season.*

Varieties of cider apple

Tremlett's Bitter: very red fruit; harvested mid-autumn; bittersweet flavour; *flowers early.*

Brown's Apple: harvested mid-autumn; sharp flavoured variety; *flowers early.*

Donald Smith

Bramley (cooking apple)

Harry Smith

James Grieve

17

Blackcurrants

Ribes nigrum (fam. *Saxifragaceae*)
Hardy deciduous shrub, with a useful life of twelve years
Size: bush about 1.5 m (5′) high and wide
Planting to harvesting time: two years
Yield: 4 kg (9 lb) average per bush

Blackcurrants are an easy soft fruit to cultivate and require a moist climate for best results. These delicious juicy berries are the richest in vitamin C of all the garden fruits and their sharp, tangy flavour has made them popular for pies, puddings and jams.

Four blackcurrant bushes at or near full cropping capacity will probably satisfy the needs of most families. It is a good idea to plant a range of varieties; this is not necessary for cross pollination, but it will spread the picking and flowering seasons, and be an insurance against a single frost causing crop failure. You can plant at any time during winter when the ground is not frozen or waterlogged, but early winter is best, so order new bushes in good time. Make sure you buy healthy two-year-old plants, preferably from ministry-certified clean stock, as supplied by most reputable nurseries. Plants which are not certified are liable to diseases, and they may give diminished yields.

Suitable site and soil

Choose a warm spot, sheltered from cold winds; this is essential because the flowers are prone to frost damage, causing a drop in yield. An open sunny aspect is preferable, but the crop will tolerate partial shade.

Blackcurrants will put up with wetter soils than most other fruits; however, the best results are to be had on deep, rich, moist well-drained sandy loams. A mildly acid soil is the best; on testing you should have a pH reading of 6 or 7, so adjust the content of the soil to give this reading.

Preparing the soil

Acid soils with a pH value of 5.5 and below require sufficient hydrated lime (or ground limestone) to raise the pH to 6.5, to be applied before planting in late autumn or winter. Never mix lime with manure or fertilizer and allow at least six weeks to elapse between working in manure and the application of lime. To

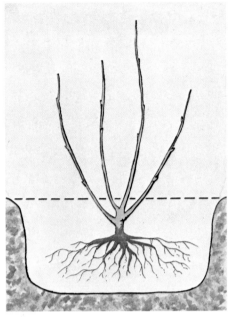

1. Prior to planting, dig the ground thoroughly to a depth of 30 cm (1′), incorporating manure.

2. Plant the bush with enough room for the roots to spread. Place the soil mark about 5 cm below ground.

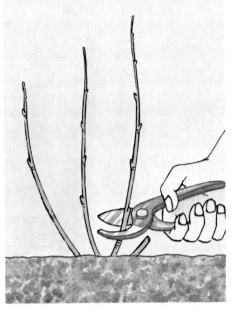

3. After planting, fill in the hole and gently heel in the soil to firm the ground around the bush.

4. Immediately after planting, use secateurs to cut back every shoot to 2.5 cm (1″) above the ground.

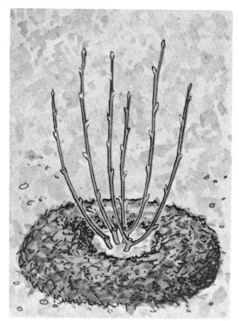

Several months after planting, work in a compound fertilizer around the roots of the bush.

Apply a mulch of well-rotted manure or garden compost to nourish the bush and help retain moisture.

raise the pH from 5.5 to 6.5 on a medium loam will require a dressing of hydrated lime at the rate of 400 g per sq m (12 oz per sq yd).

On soils which are alkaline, such as those occurring in chalk and limestone districts, where the soil pH is 7-7.5, be sure to work in plenty of peat before and during planting.

Before digging over the ground, dispose of perennial weeds, such as nettles, thistles, docks and couch grass. Fork them out carefully and remove them from the site. Weedkillers can be used, provided you allow sufficient time so that no harmful residues remain at planting time.

Dig the ground over, to a full spade depth of 30 cm (1'), about six weeks if possible before planting and work in manure, compost or leafmould at the time of digging. The rate of dressing of organic matter should be one wheelbarrow load per 1.7 sq m (2 sq yd) of ground. If this sounds rather heavy, bear in mind

that these plants occupy the site for a number of years.

Blackcurrants respond well to generous dressings of nitrogenous feeds, so, following the digging in of organic matter, provide extra plant food by forking into the surface a dressing of 45 g per sq m ($1\frac{1}{2}$ oz per sq yd) each of sterilized bonemeal and hoof-and-horn meal, together with 30 g per sq m (1 oz per sq yd) of sulphate of potash. Alternatively, apply a dressing of general garden fertilizer at 120 g per sq m (4 oz per sq yd). The analysis of the general fertilizer should be approximately 7% nitrogen, 7% phosphate, 12% potassium.

Planting

Space the plants at 1.8 m (6 ft) apart. Dig a planting hole big enough to spread the roots out in their natural directions without being cramped. Blackcurrants, when established, have a number of main stems arising at or just below

Bushes can be protected from frosts by a covering of heavy polythene.

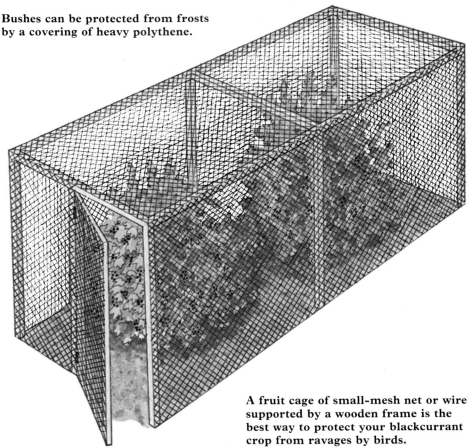

A fruit cage of small-mesh net or wire supported by a wooden frame is the best way to protect your blackcurrant crop from ravages by birds.

High-yielding blackcurrant bushes are an excellent investment. Be sure to leave adequate space for development when you first plant them.

ground level, unlike gooseberries, red currants and white currants which grow on a leg or single stem. To encourage this habit of producing vigorous stems low down, bushes should be planted 2.5-5 cm (1-2″) deeper than they were in the nursery. The nursery level will be indictated by a soil mark, where the stem changes colour.

When each bush is placed in its planting hole, work in the soil around the roots and firm it with your heel.

Immediately after planting cut every shoot to within 2.5 cm (1″) of the ground to just above the first or second visible growth bud. This cutting back ensures that the bushes develop good root systems and strong vigorous stems, but they will not produce fruit the first year. If there have been some hard frosts after planting and the bushes and soil have loosened as a result, be sure to firm the soil around the roots again.

Aftercare

Water the plants early in the season following planting if the weather is dry. Blackcurrants need moisture more than most fruits. Mulching to conserve moisture and smother weeds should be carried out early. Remove weeds and keep them under control as soon as they appear, to prevent them competing with bushes for moisture and to reduce the risk of other hosts for pests and diseases.

Blackcurrants grow and crop better with generous dressings of manure or compost, or peat and fertilizer. In early spring each year, scatter and work in 30 g per sq m (1 oz per sq yd) of sulphate of ammonia and 15 g sq m ($\frac{1}{2}$ oz per sq yd) of sulphate of potash over the bed. Where the soil is acid, use nitro-chalk instead of sulphate of ammonia.

Working in the fertilizer can be carried out with a rake if the soil surface is crumbly and friable. If the surface has

PRUNING

Pruning from the second year is to encourage new wood, as this bears the most fruit the next year, and to build up a good bush shape. Prune to the ground, or to a low-growing shoot, and ignore new growth at the tip of old wood. Low-growing branches, crossing branches and those which are diseased are cut out first, followed by those branches in the centre of the bush, to let in light and air. Finally, a proportion of old wood is cut to a low shoot, or is removed entirely.

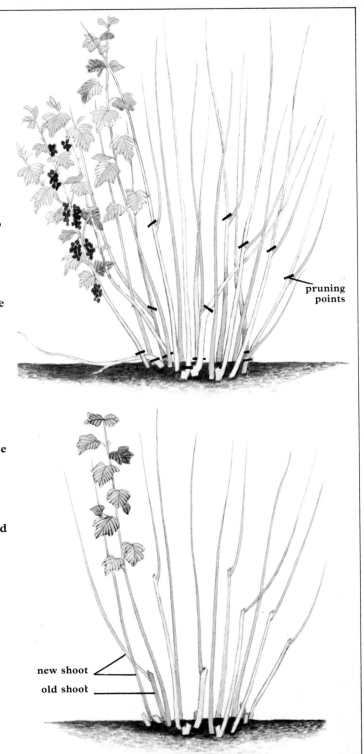

pruning points

new shoot

old shoot

become rather compacted after the winter rains, then use a hand cultivator or garden fork to do two jobs in one, to loosen the surface and work in the fertilizer before a mulch is applied.

Mulching will feed the bushes, besides its other functions. A mulch of manure or compost laid on top of the soil should be applied at the rate of one wheelbarrow-load to 2.5 sq m (3 sq yd). If no manure is available, double the quantities of fertilizers and mulch with moist peat or pulverized tree bark.

Frost protection

The greenish white flowers are borne in hanging clusters of four to twelve, or even more in early to mid-spring.

To protect the bushes from frost, cover the bushes at night with hessian, cloth or plastic attached to a light framework.

Pruning

In the winter following planting, little pruning will be needed, but any weak growths can be cut back to the first bud above ground level. Immediately after the first harvest, the second winter after planting, pruning should be carried out.

Blackcurrants bear most of their fruit on the new shoots produced the previous summer, so the aim of pruning is to encourage the growth of strong new wood from the base of the plant. Most of the new shoots will be retained, and some of the older wood which also bears a quota of fruit. First cut away low-growing growths which hang down to the ground, also any which are dead or obviously diseased, and any that are crossing or awkwardly placed. If the centre of the bush is crowded, remove some of the shoots there to let in light and air.

Finally, remove about one-fifth of the older wood that remains. Make your cuts above a good new low-growing shoot or close to the ground to encourage new growth lower down, and ignore promising growth at the tips of these shoots.

When the bushes are well established,

after about four seasons, remove roughly one-third of the old wood each winter. Where growth is very vigorous remove less, but if it is weak and needs stimulating, then prune more severely.

Harvesting

The bushes will need some protection, by the use of netting or a wire cage, from the ravages of birds as the fruits ripen. Fruits are ready for picking when they are black or nearly so; the time of ripening depends on the variety you choose. Always pick when the fruit is dry; wet fruit goes mouldy very quickly. For quickness, berries can be stripped off their stalks using a kitchen fork, but fruits picked off a truss or cluster are less likely to go mouldy and will keep for four or five days in cool conditions. Some varieties do not ripen evenly so that on the cluster of fruits some berries are ready for picking while others are still green. In this event stripping off fruits with a fork is not very practical.

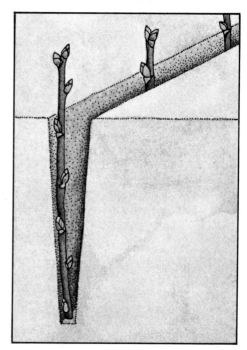

To propagate plants, take cuttings in mid-autumn and insert them in the ground with some buds below the soil.

24

Pat Brindley

Boskoop Giant

A – Z Collection

The Raven

Varieties

Propagation

Hardwood cuttings, an easy and convenient means of propagation, should be taken in mid-autumn from healthy bushes. Under no circumstances should cuttings be taken from diseased bushes to replace those about to be destroyed.

Cuttings are prepared from shoots of ripening wood, about 20-25 cm (8-10″) long, cut just below a bud. Dig V-shaped trenches about 15 cm (6″) deep. Some sharp sand placed in the bottom of the 'V' trench is a useful aid to rooting. Put in the cuttings, leaving two or more buds above ground, and spaced at 15-20 cm (6-8″) apart. These shoots are then firmed in. Unlike gooseberries and red currants, blackcurrant cuttings do not have any of the buds rubbed off before inserting into the ground.

By the following autumn, the cuttings will be ready for transplanting into their new quarters.

Softwood cuttings (i.e. immature shoot tips) about 7.5 cm (3″) long taken in late spring to early summer and rooted in a shaded frame, is an alternative method of propagation. When the cuttings are rooted, increase ventilation gradually until the frame is removed.

These fall into a number of categories, but are usually classified according to the time of fruiting, namely—early, mid-season, and late varieties. However, the time and habit of fruiting differ within those groups. Some varieties, such as *Seabrook's Black* and *Boskoop Giant* may be set back by frost (possibly because they lack leafy cover for the flowers).

The list is by no means exhaustive, but these varieties are well tried and proven by commercial growers and amateurs. Most have some resistance to diseases.

Early varieties

Mendip Cross: large spreading bush; flowers mid-season; berries medium to large, heaviest cropper of the early sorts; moderately resistant to leaf spot.

Boskoop Giant: a very old, but well tried variety; vigorous habit, between *The Raven* and *Mendip Cross*. Flowers early; large berries, well spaced and easy to pick. The earliest variety to ripen, but tends to have a lighter crop. Moderate resistance to leaf spot.

Tor Cross: similar to *Mendip Cross;* flowers mid-season to late; better quality fruit than *Mendip Cross* and develops

Wellington XXX

Blacksmith

two or three days later; moderate to good resistance to leaf spot.

Mid-season

Seabrooks Black: medium upright growth; late flowering, good for exposed or northern areas; berries medium-sized, fruits about seven days later than *Mendip Cross*; moderately resistant to leaf spot.

The Raven: largest bush of all, open nature, but stiff stems; flowers early, but well protected by the foliage; large sweet fruit of even size and thin skinned. Outstanding for juice and flavouring; not susceptible to leaf spot.

Wellington XXX: open habit, inclined to droop with a heavy crop; flowers early, liable to be damaged by frosts and cold winds in exposed sites. Fruit of good size and quality; crops well in milder areas; susceptible to leaf spot.

Blacksmith: very vigorous, makes a rather uneven bush; flowers late; prolific cropper, large berries at base of clusters, small at the ends; fruit hidden in foliage. Short season, ripens few days before *Baldwin*; moderate resistance to leaf spot.

Brodtorp: a newer variety of considerable promise, but requires further trials before a full assessment is given.

Late Varieties

Baldwin: a very old variety and a good cropper; makes a dense upright bush; flowers mid-season; medium-sized fruits, easy to pick and thick skinned; ripens evenly; berries hang well unless the foliage is poor; succeeds best in mild areas (e.g. southern and western England) where it crops regularly and heavily; stands closer planting; prone to leaf spot.

Westwick Choice: very compact; flowers mid to late season; berries large and firm; ripens a few days after *Baldwin* and hangs well; more resistant to leaf spot than *Baldwin*.

Amos Black: vigorous, upright unbranched stems and dark green foliage; flowers late season; large berries on short branches; variable cropper; moderate resistance to leaf spot.

Daniels September: vigorous open bush, tends to have characteristic leaf mottle; flowers late, after *Baldwin*; two forms of fruit develop, early and late; the latter is the desirable form; large, thick skinned fruits, hang late for about fourteen days after *Baldwin*; moderate resistance to leaf spot.

Malvern Cross: similar habit to *Wellington XXX*; flowers late season; well berried, but tip fruits are small.

Pests & Diseases

Unfortunately, blackcurrants are very prone to attack by a variety of insects, viruses and fungi. However, if you make sure that your plants come from certified stock and follow a sensible preventive spray programme, you have an excellent chance of a healthy crop. It is particularly important to protect your plants from infection by blackcurrant gall mite. Spray with 1% solution of lime-sulphur when the first flowers open, and repeat three weeks later. Malathion or derris sprays are useful against aphids, capsids, blackcurrant sawflies, leaf midge and red spider mites. In all cases, spray exactly at the time stated, and never spray when the blossom is in full bloom.

Blackcurrant gall mite/Big bud: infection with blackcurrant gall mite is responsible for the disease 'big bud'. The gall mite also transmits reversion virus (see below). These mites are minute in size, and thousands of them can be found in a single infected bud. The infected bud then swells prematurely and becomes less pointed (hence the name 'big bud'). There is no completely effective control but spraying twice each spring with lime sulphur,

1% strength, at the rate of $\frac{1}{3}$ litre to 27 litres of water ($\frac{1}{2}$ pt to 6 gallons of water) is a useful measure. Apply the solution as the first flowers open, and again three weeks later. Prune branches which show signs of big bud on slightly infected bushes. Badly infected bushes should be dug up and burned.

Reversion virus: this incurable virus disease is carried by the blackcurrant gall mite. It is difficult to diagnose leaf reversion in its early stages because the infected plant may appear no different from a healthy one, except for a reduction in cropping. In late spring or early summer, closely examine the leaves of those plants which have cropped poorly. If the plants have reversion virus, the leaf structure may have changed. Healthy leaves have five or more veins on either side of the centre rib of the lobe opposite the leaf stalk. Reverted leaves have less than five. Infected plants will never recover. Remove and burn them. Plant healthy replacement stock on a different site well removed from possible sources of infection.

Aphids: the first sign to look for is stunted leaf growth, leaf curling and leaf distortion. Cotton wool-like grubs on

GUIDE TO BLACKCURRANT TROUBLES

Symptoms	Probable cause
Unnaturally large, swollen buds	Blackcurrant gall mite
Leaf veins reduced in number, little fruit produced	Leaf reversion virus
Stunted growth, leaf curling and distortion	Aphids
Whitish orange maggots, twisted or folded leaves	Blackcurrant leaf midge
Green and black caterpillars, foliage stripped	Blackcurrant sawfly
Green, winged insects causing disfiguration of leaves, fruits, shoots	Capsids
Minute red or brown mites, yellow, stunted growth	Red spider mite
Buds fail to open in spring, long bare branches	Eelworm
Brown spots on leaves from mid-spring onward	Blackcurrant leaf spot
Yellow pustules on undersides of leaves in early summer	Blackcurrant rust
White felty growths on young leaves, fruits and shoots, growths later turning brown	American gooseberry mildew
Delicate powdery mould on underside of leaves	European gooseberry mould

the roots of the infected plants are due to currant root aphids. To control aphids, spray in mid-winter with a tar-oil spray. As soon as the first flowers open, spray with malathion, thoroughly wetting the undersides of the leaves.

Blackcurrant leaf midge: This pest usually appears in its larval stage as whitish orange maggots which cause the leaves to twist and become folded. *Seabrook's Black, Wellington* and *Baldwin* are the most susceptible varieties of blackcurrants. Spray with malathion at the open flower stage.

Blackcurrant sawfly: the green and black caterpillars of this insect will quickly strip a plant of foliage. The damage is usually done on the underside or in the centre of the infected bush. If the caterpillars appear, pick them off by hand, or give an extra spray with derris or mathathion.

Common green capsid: this insect's over wintering eggs hatch out when the flowers are about to open. The emergent winged capsid will attack other garden crops as well as blackcurrants. It sucks the sap from the growing shoot tips; scars are formed and later the leaves become puckered and distorted. Again, a spray of malathion before the flowers

George Hyde

Blackcurrants showing the enlarged buds of 'Big Bud' trouble, caused by gall mites.

open will control these pests. Treat the eggs with tar oil sprays.

Red spider mite: these are minute red or brown mites which suck the sap from leaves, eventually weakening the plant. A sign to watch for is the rapid bronzing of leaves. Spray with malathion at the first open flower stage.

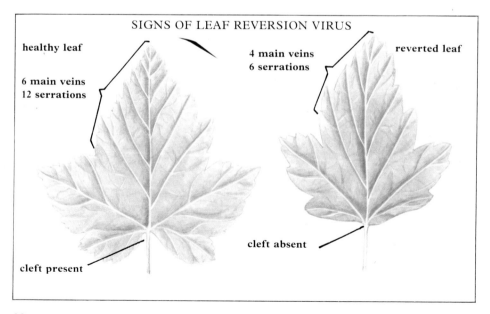

SIGNS OF LEAF REVERSION VIRUS

healthy leaf

6 main veins
12 serrations

4 main veins
6 serrations

reverted leaf

cleft absent

cleft present

Royal Horticultural Gardens, Wisley

Severely distorted leaves caused by an attack of the common green capsid.

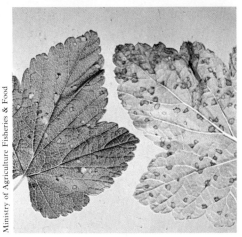

Ministry of Agriculture Fisheries & Food

Blackcurrant leaves displaying a mild (left) and severe (right) leaf spot disease.

Ministry of Agriculture Fisheries & Food

White felty growths on plants suffering from American gooseberry mildew.

Eelworm: damage from this pest is usually worse after a wet season. Buds will fail to open in spring, leaving long, bare branches. *Daniel's Black* and *Westwick* are particularly susceptible blackcurrant varieties. Eelworm is best controlled by avoiding planting on diseased ground, especially following potato crops. This problem is rare.

Blackcurrant leaf spot: this fungus can be fairly damaging unless kept in check. It is likely to occur in higher rain fall areas and in wet seasons. Brown spots appear on the leaves from late spring onwards if the attack is severe, the bush can be badly weakened. Premature leaf fall is an indication of infection by leaf spot. Spray the infected plants with copper fungicide, zineb or thiram immediately after flowering and three more times at four-weekly intervals; you can also apply Bordeaux mixture, if the disease was severe in the last season, but only after picking.

Blackcurrant rust: the symptoms of this disease are yellow, raised pustules on the undersides of the leaves in early summer. Fungicide sprays of copper, thiram of zineb will control blackcurrant rust.

American gooseberry mildew/ European gooseberry mildew: the American mildew is the more dangerous of the two; its symptoms are white felty growths on the young leaves, fruits and shoots. In summer and autumn, the fungal growth becomes brown and felt like. The European mildew shows itself as a delicate, powdery mould on the undersides of the leaves. Both are controlled by lime sulphur or dinocap sprays before the flowers open. Cut out any diseased shoots.

29

Gooseberries

Ribes grossularia (fam. *Grossulariaceae*)
Hardy deciduous shrub with a
useful life of 12 to 20 years
Size: 1 m (3′) high; 1.2-1.5 m (4-5′) wide
Planting to harvesting time: 2-3 years
Yield: 3.5-7 kg (8-15 lb) per bush and more

Gooseberries are easy to grow and are probably the best soft fruit for a small garden. Their cultivation needs are moderate, they give a large amount of fruit for the area they cover, and a well-tended bush will go on cropping for twenty years or more. Three or four gooseberry bushes will be ample to supply the needs of most households. However, gooseberries are self-fertile, so you can grow a single bush in your garden with good results. Gooseberries are very tolerant of exposure and are occasionally grown as windbreaks to protect less hardy crops, though strong winds at flowering time will discourage pollinating insects. They are more shade tolerant than other soft fruits, so gooseberries will thrive in town gardens where other soft fruits fail.

There are many varieties of gooseberry available; if you plant several bushes you can extend the season of cropping from early summer through to early autumn. Gooseberries are usually first picked when the fruits are small and green. These unripe thinnings are cooked and served in pies or puddings or preserved for future use. Ripe gooseberries are highly valued as a dessert fruit, and are delicious when eaten raw. First class dessert gooseberries are seldom seen in shops, so it would be well worthwhile for the amateur gardener to have at least one bush in the garden. Ripe dessert gooseberries can be yellow, white, green or red. The Worcester-berry, a gooseberry hybrid and not, as often thought, a cross between a goose-berry and a blackcurrant, has fairly small, blue-black, gooseberry-like fruit, and it is cultivated in the same way.

Gooseberries are usually grown as spiney shrubs on a single short stem like a tiny tree, although cordons, espaliers and standards are available. A goose-berry grown as a standard is particularly suitable for planting in pots if you have a paved terrace, courtyard or balcony. They make attractive features and will carry good crops if properly cared for.

Suitable site and soil
The best soil for gooseberries is a well-drained loam containing plenty of potash and nitrogen; gooseberries, more than

Gooseberries are best protected from attacks by birds if they are grown in fruit cages.

other soft fruits, are very particular about soil conditions. Generally, light soils or sandy gravel are not suitable because they lack nutrients and tend to dry out in hot weather. Chalk soils are unsuitable because they heat up in the summer, and gooseberries need a cool moist root run. Whatever the soil, it must be moisture retentive because the fruits will not swell if moisture is lacking. If the soil is too rich and fertile, however, sappy weak growth and poor crops will result. Some varieties of gooseberry are more tolerant of difficult soil conditions than others: *Whinham's Industry* is recommended for heavy soils, *Lancer* for light soils. Unfortunately, *Leveller,* which is highly prized for its delicious

dessert berries, needs near perfect soil conditions to crop well.

When selecting a site, much depends on the general geographic location. The best flavoured gooseberries are grown in cooler areas. This is because the berries are less liable to be ripened prematurely by hot sun and they have time to mature slowly. In Britain, the counties of Cheshire and Lancashire and nearby areas have appeared to be particularly good locations.

Some varieties such as *Whinhams Industry* are shade tolerant. Rows of gooseberry bushes are sometimes grown between young apple trees; and are dug up after 15-20 years, when the trees are reaching maturity. Gooseberries, like

31

1. Dig in well-rotted manure, leaf mould, garden compost or moist peat. Make sure all weeds are removed.

2. Plant in autumn, in a hole about 60 cm (2′) in diameter. Spread the roots out and replace soil firmly.

3. Heel in the soil around the bush, but do not compact it too much or rain will lie on the surface.

red currants, can be grown against north-facing walls and fences in gardens where space is limited. Cordons are the best shape to grow against fences or on their own as a boundary between gardens.

Generally, a sunny site will give a better flavoured crop. In full sun, gooseberries should be grown as bushes so the branches help shade the fruit hanging beneath.

Avoid windy sites, because cold winds prevent insects from pollinating them in early spring. Gooseberries are hardier than plums, apples and pears, and they will probably produce a moderate crop even if the flowers have been frosted. A frost-free site is better, though.

The site must be well drained, because gooseberries will not tolerate any water-logging. Avoid low-lying sites on heavy soil because they tend to be badly drained and form frost pockets in winter.

Soil preparation and planting

Gooseberries fruit on both old and new wood, so it is important that the plant makes good strong annual growth. The best way to ensure this is by preparing the soil adequately prior to planting in early autumn. Ideally, the soil should have been under cultivation for several seasons; if the site is newly cultivated, it is best to double-dig it.

For all soil types, dig into the top spit well-rotted farmyard manure or garden compost, moist peat or leafmould, remembering that the peat will not have any nutrient value. Light soils will then be made more moisture retentive, heavier soils more friable. Also apply sulphate of potash at this time, at the rate of 25 g per sq m ($\frac{3}{4}$ oz per sq yd), forking it lightly into the soil. Make sure the area is completely weed-free. Once couch grass, bindweed or docks grow up into a gooseberry bush they are impossible to eradicate.

If you are buying gooseberry bushes, make sure they come from a reputable source; try to get two or three-year old bushes.

The best time to plant gooseberries is in early autumn, so that the bushes have plenty of time to settle down and become established before making spring growth. If you are planting more than one bush, the distance between planting depends on the variety and the shape grown. Normally, strong growing bushes of varieties such as *Lancer*, *Lancashire Lad* and *White Lion*, should be planted 1.8 m (6′) apart. Less vigorous varieties can be planted 1.5 m (5′) apart. Single cordons should be 30 cm (1′) apart; double and triple cordons and espalier-trained gooseberries should be 90 cm (3′) apart. If you are planting more than one row, leave at least 2.4 m (8′) between rows.

Before planting, remove all buds and suckers below the main shoots. If there are any suckers on the roots, take these off also. Gooseberries are usually grown on a single leg, or clear stem, about 15 cm (6″) high. You may have to trim off the top-most roots (very carefully) and plant the bush a little higher than the nursery soil mark, to get a good leg. This also helps keep down suckering.

Plant the bushes firmly, and not too deeply. Do not compact the soil too much, or rain will lie in puddles on the surface. Trained specimens should be staked when they are planted. Standard gooseberries will need strong stakes at least 1.2 m (4′) tall.

Cultivation

Gooseberries benefit greatly from feeding and mulching annually; greater yields will result if you follow these routines.

In spring or late summer, apply well-rotted garden compost, at the rate of one barrowload per 10 sq m (11 sq yd). This encourages the formation of fibrous feeding roots, and increases crop production. Mulching also helps to keep weeds down and conserve soil moisture.

Because gooseberries need more potash than other soft fruits, they should have annual application of sulphate of potash at the rate of 20-30 g per sq m ($\frac{3}{4}$-1

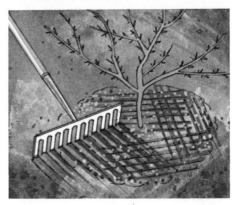

1. Each year in late winter or early spring apply sulphate of potash before mulching, and rake it in.

2. Mulch annually with well-rotted manure or compost to encourage the formation of fibrous feeding roots.

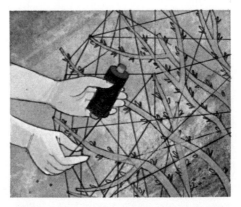

3. If birds are a problem, thread black cotton through the branches in mid-autumn as a deterrent.

oz per sq yd). This should be done in later winter or early spring, but if the edges of the leaves look scorched, brown and fall prematurely the plant is suffering from potash deficiency—apply sulphate of potash at the higher of the above rates immediately and water in. Sandy and gravelly soils are usually deficient in potash, so make sure you apply a potash fertilizer regularly. Ashes from the bonfire contain potash, and a mulch of these can provide additional potash.

Nitrogen is also necessary, to promote strong growth. However, if too much nitrogen is applied, sappy weak growth will result, with an increased risk of mildew. Usually, a mulch of garden compost in spring is sufficient. Every third year apply a dressing of super-phosphate at the rate of 90-120 g per sq m (3-4 oz per sq yd) with the potash.

In winter check the plants frequently; firm down any lifted by frost. To reduce the risk of damage by frost, cover the bushes 'in early and mid-spring with muslin or fine netting.

Birds, usually bullfinches and sparrows, tend to peck the buds out from late autumn to late winter. The variety *Leveller* seems particularly vulnerable to bird attacks. If the fruits are not grown in cages, the best method of protection is winding black cotton thread round the shoots and branches after leaf fall. If your garden is very vulnerable to bird damage, it is best to delay pruning until bud break in spring. In early spring, when bud-breaks occurs, and you find that a shoot or shoots have been largely stripped of buds, cut them right back to the first strong bud near the base of the shoot; a badly-stripped shoot will not recover.

Watering is necessary in dry weather from late spring to mid-summer, otherwise the fruit will not swell and the leaves may scorch. This is particularly important for sandy or other very free-draining soils.

Water the plants at the rate of 20 L per sq m (4½ gal per sq yd).

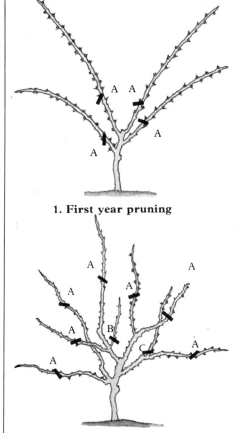

1. First year pruning

2. Second year pruning

1. *The first pruning consists of cutting back three or four strong shoots to an outward pointing bud, three or four buds from the base (A). Remove weak or badly placed buds.*

2. *One year later, cut back 5-8 strong shoots to half their length, to an outward pointing bud (A). Shorten smaller sideshoots to one bud from the base (B); remove completely any weak or badly placed shoots (C). When pruning to form the framework of the bush, aim for an open-centred bush.*

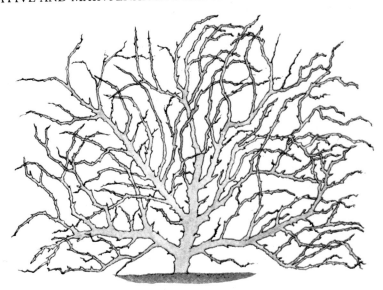

Established gooseberry bush (unpruned)

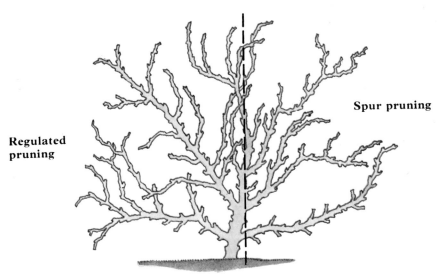

Spur pruning

Regulated pruning

Established gooseberry bush (pruned)

There are two methods of pruning an established bush; regulated and spur pruning. The former consists of removing overcrowded, weak and old wood, pruning branch leaders back by a quarter, and pruning one-year-old shoots by 7.5 cm (3"). To spur prune, cut back all sideshoots to one or two buds, to encourage the formation of fruiting spurs. Spur pruning results in larger, but fewer, gooseberries.

If you removed all the weeds before the bushes were planted, you should have little trouble with weeds later. Should weeding be necessary, however, hand weed or hoe lightly. Never dig between the bushes or hoe deeply because you may damage the fibrous surface feeding roots. Mulching is a good way of keeping weeds down. Watch for brambles in particular seeding in the middle of the bushes.

Check for suckers growing up from the roots and carefully cut off any you find. If the suckers are left, the bush will lose its shape and be difficult to pick from.

Pruning

Gooseberries can be trained into a number of shapes. Although the bush form is the most commonly seen, gooseberries can be grown as single, double or triple cordons, as espaliers and as standards, and even as fans. You may be able to buy a standard gooseberry from your local nurseryman; it will probably have been grafted on to a rootstock of golden currant (*Ribes aureum*). It is quite easy to train a standard yourself. Remove all but one strong straight shoot from a new bush and train it vertically until it has reached about 1.2 m (4'). Remove all the lower side shoots from the stem, leaving the top four or five buds to form the branching head of the gooseberry, which is then pruned as though it was an ordinary bush.

Cordon trained gooseberries are particularly suitable for growing in rows against a wall or where room is scarce. Single cordons are trained by cutting back all side shoots to leave one bud only on each, and cutting the leader back each year to leave about 15 cm (6″) of new growth until the desired height is reached, about 1.5-1.8 m (5-6'). Then cut away the whole of any leading shoot each year, so that the spurs lower down continue to be strong. Double cordons are slightly more difficult. Begin by cutting back the main stem to leave two

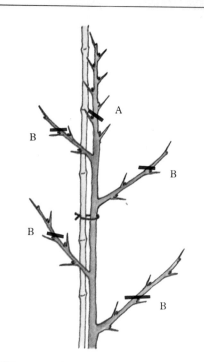

Winter pruning consists of shortening the leading shoot to leave one third of its new growth (A), and pruning laterals back to three buds (B). Pruning laterals encourages the formation of fruiting spurs. In areas where bird damage to gooseberry buds is severe, leave pruning until early spring.

buds pointed in opposite directions, about 22 cm (9″) from the ground. Train the shoots which grow out from these buds at an angle of 45° at first, later gradually lowering them to the horizontal. Tie these horizontal shoots on to wires, and then cut them back to leave one bud on the upper side of each. These two buds will produce the vertical framework of the cordon. The formative pruning of specially trained forms is done in early winter unless birds are likely to be a problem when it should be done at bud-break. The early pruning of gooseberry bushes is aimed at establishing a strong open framework able to carry a heavy crop. Once this framework has been formed, there are two methods of maintenance pruning. Regulated

PRUNING ESTABLISHED GOOSEBERRY CORDONS

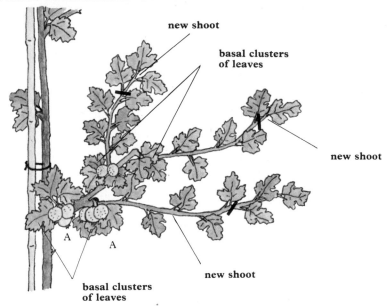

new shoot

basal clusters
of leaves

new shoot

new shoot

A   A

basal clusters
of leaves

In mid-summer, prune back laterals to 5 or 6 leaves, not counting the basal clusters (A). This pruning encourages the formation of fruit buds. As American gooseberry mildew appears first on the tips, Regulated pruning at this time helps to control the disease.

If the cordon has reached the desired height, you can cut back the leading shoot during routine summer pruning. Sometimes, sucker-like shoots appear near the base of the cordons; cut these off cleanly as soon as they are seen, as they will drain the cordon of energy needed to produce the fruit.

pruning ensures a large quantity of berries, perhaps for freezing or bottling, where perfection and size are not so important. If you want fewer, but larger and higher quality berries, for exhibition or dessert, spur pruning is the best method (see diagram). Spur pruning is also recommended for bushes growing on light soils or where growth is poor.

Growing standard gooseberries in containers

This method is suitable if you have a paved terrace or courtyard. Select a pot 30 cm (12″) in diameter and 30 cm (12″) deep to start with; as the plant grows on you will have to repot into a larger pot, say 35 cm × 35 cm (14″ × 14″). Line the bottom of the pot with a layer of drainage material, such as large stones or broken pieces of clay pots or brick. Then put in a layer of good loam mixed with an equal part of well-rotted garden compost, or use John Innes potting compost No. 3. Carefully spread the roots of the plant out over this layer, and fill the pot with more of the mixture until the top of the soil is 2.5 cm (1″) beneath the rim of the pot. Water in well. Potting is best done in mid-autumn or early spring. Remember that plants in pots dry out very quickly in hot weather, so water the pots frequently— daily in very hot weather.

Do not feed the plant for the first year, as it is still becoming established. Thereafter, feed with liquid fertilizer when the fruits are swelling. If you live in a warm area or if your garden is fairly sheltered, you can leave the pot outside all year round without protection; otherwise plunge the pot in a sheltered border for the winter and mulch heavily, or put some form of lagging round the pot and over the compost surface to protect the roots from hard frost.

Propagation

There are three methods of propagating gooseberries: layering, cuttings and seeds. Layering is the easiest method, and probably the one most suited to the amateur gardener. Peg down suitably placed shoots in early summer and cover with a thin layer of soil about halfway along their length. By late autumn the rooted layer should be severed from the parent plant and moved to its permanent position. Unfortunately, bushes propagated by layering are less symmetrical than those raised by cuttings; they tend to sucker more, and it is difficult to get a clean leg.

The main problem with propagation by cuttings is that gooseberry cuttings do not root easily. If you try this method, prepare more cuttings than you need, as there will probably be some failures. If all the cuttings root successfully, you can share them with friends or neighbours.

One of the main reasons for failure of cuttings is the drying out of the cut end.

Cuttings must not be left around while you prepare the site in which to root them; once the sap has dried the cutting will not root. Dig the trench beforehand in early autumn, selecting a warm and sheltered site. It should be V-shaped in section, and 22 cm (9″) deep. If you are digging more than one trench, make them at least 60 cm (2′) apart. Then spread a 7.5 cm (3″) layer of sand mixed with a little moist peat in the bottom of the trench.

Cuttings should be taken while some of the leaves are still on the bush; the earlier in autumn they are taken, the better provided the wood is ripe. Use only one-year-old shoots (these are lighter in colour than old wood) about 25 cm (10″) long; the shoots should be straight and thick but not sappy. Remove the top 2.5 cm (1″) tip, cutting just above a leaf cluster or bud. The bottom cut should be made just below a leaf cluster or bud. Rub off the lower buds leaving about four or five buds on the upper part of the shoot. Branches will develop from these buds, and the lower portion will form the leg.

Dip the bottom 5 cm (2″) of the cutting in hormone rooting powder, and then insert the cutting firmly against one side of the trench so that about half the cutting is above the soil surface.

PROPAGATING FROM CUTTINGS

1. Take cuttings of one-year-old shoots in autumn; plant immediately in trenches; space cuttings 15 cm (6″) apart.

2. The next autumn, rub out any suckers (A) and cut back side-shoots by half (B). Cut off terminal shoot (C).

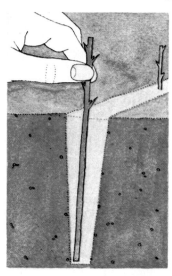
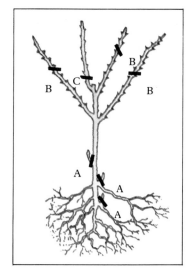

A standard gooseberry is very easy to train and makes an attractive feature in the garden. They are also very suitable for growing in large pots if you have a paved terrace, courtyard or balcony.

Cuttings should be spaced 15 cm (6″) apart. Press the soil sufficiently firmly around the cuttings so they do not feel loose when given a gentle tug, and make sure the soil does not dry out. Keep the ground well weeded. If you have extra cloches available, it is a good idea to cover the cuttings during the worst of the winter months.

The following autumn, one year later, rub out any unwanted buds or suckers on the stem and roots and replant the rooted cutting in its permanent position.

If you do not mind waiting three or four seasons for the first fruit, gooseberries can be grown quite easily from seed. Sow seeds taken from a fully ripe berry in a 1.2 cm (½″) deep furrow. Keep it weeded and well watered in dry weather. The following spring transplant them so they are 60 cm (2′) apart. If you have planted out more than one row, the rows should be at least 60 cm (2′) apart. The following spring transplant them out again, into their permanent positions. You will find that the seedlings vary greatly in quality; discard all but the best.

Harvesting

Harvesting is done in several stages; early thinnings are useful for tarts and jam-making, while the final crops of large, fully ripe fruit are usually eaten fresh. Start picking late in spring when the fruits are about the size of peas. Thinning at this stage leads to larger fruit later on. Because the colours of the different varieties do not appear until the fruits are nearly ripe, all thinnings at this stage will be green. Pick the berries off the bush with a quick jerk; in this way the fruit can be removed from the plant without damaging the spur.

The first picking should be done all over the bush, so that the remaining berries are evenly distributed. The thinned fruit should be at least 3.7 cm ($1\frac{1}{2}''$) apart. The next picking should be done from the centre of the bush and from lower branches. Fruits in these positions are unlikely to ripen completely, because of shading. The best placed fruits on the outer branches are then left on the bush to mature fully, and picked for dessert use when soft and ripe. To obtain the best flavour, pick these dessert gooseberries during the afternoon or early evening, while they are still warm from the sun. If possible, avoid picking while the weather is wet.

Exhibition tips

For exhibition work it is best to spur prune your bush (see *Pruning* above) to get good size fruits of the finest quality. When the fruits begin to set, apply weekly applications of manure water until just before the show date. If there has been a very heavy set of fruit, thin them after they have begun to swell..

Gooseberries, like other soft fruit, should be shown with a stalk still attached. Thirty berries is the usual number called for. They should all be of the same variety and as uniform in appearance and size as possible. Judging is divided into two categories: ripe and unripe gooseberries. Ripe fruits should be fully ripe and of good colour, unripe fruits should be large and fresh.

Pests & Diseases

Gooseberries are relatively pest and disease free, given proper cultivation. It is a good idea, if you have had insect trouble, to spray them with a tar oil wash in winter. Do this when you spray plums and redcurrants. Then inspect your plants in spring and early summer for signs of attacks and spray or dust with pesticides in severe cases.

Caterpillars: the caterpillars of the gooseberry sawfly are very destructive and in bad years can quickly strip a plant of foliage. It is a particularly troublesome pest because there are three generations of sawfly in one season. For this reason it is important to completely kill off the first generation of caterpillars when they hatch out in spring. They eat small holes in the leaves; eventually the whole leaf is eaten except for the main veins and midrib. In mild attacks, pick them off by hand or spread out sacking beneath the bush and shake them out. If the attack is severe, handpick as much as possible as soon as the caterpillars appear, and then spray with derris. Similar damage is done by the black, white and yellow caterpillar of the magpie moth. Treatment is the same.

Gooseberry red spider mite: these do most damage in mid and late spring,

The caterpillars of the gooseberry sawfly can quickly strip a plant of all leaves.

when the weather is fine. They suck the sap from the undersurface of the leaves and are especially troublesome during warm, sunny springs. The leaves become pale or bronze-coloured and may fall prematurely; any fruits which form will be small and unappetizing. In general the mites migrate to the bushes in spring from apple trees and buildings; spray just after flowering with dimethoate or malathion to control them.

Birds: these are particularly troublesome in some gardens; in winter they peck out the dormant buds. If you cannot grow the bushes in fruit cages, twine cotton thread through the branches; alternatively, delay pruning until bud-break in spring (see *Cultivation* above). Harmless bird repellant sprays can also be used, containing quassia, thiram, anthroquinone and other substances unpleasant-tasting to birds.

Capsids: these pests are much more troublesome some years than others. They suck the sap from young leaves and the tips of the new growing shoots. Leaves damaged by capsids are covered with tiny pin pricks and later become distorted, tattered and browned. Fruits and flowers attacked by capsids will be mis-shaped and badly discoloured. If they appeared the previous season, as a precaution spray just after the flowering stage with malathion.

Greenfly: these tiny green 'plant lice' infest the tips of the shoots and new leaves in spring, and can result in serious damage. The new shoots will cease to grow and be stunted and distorted; sideshoots may be produced lower down whose growth is weak. Remove the worst affected tips and spray at once with derris, bioresmethrin or malathion, repeating if necessary. Remember not to spray during the day at flowering time.

Die back: this is caused by the fungus *Botrytis cinerea,* or grey mould. The main symptom is the sudden death of a whole branch or branches, often in full leaf. If the fungus attacks the main stem, the whole plant will die. Infected leaves will turn yellow and then almost white along the margins; they later turn brown and wither. Infection usually enters the bush through a wound or pruning snag. Make sure you prune correctly and paint over large wounds with fungicidal paint. If the bush is only moderately infected, cut back into living wood and burn the infected branches. If a bush is badly infected, dig it up and burn it. Plants grown in poor soils are the most susceptible, so take precautions.

American gooseberry mildew: this infection is probably the most serious gooseberry disease. The symptoms are first: white powdery patches on the young leaves as they unfold, and on the

Donald Smith

Royal Horticultural Society, Wisley, Surrey

These pale, powdery growths indicate American gooseberry mildew.

These leaves are infected with leaf spot, a disease most likely to occur in wet summers.

GUIDE TO GOOSEBERRY TROUBLES

Symptoms	Probable cause
Small holes in leaves; later entire leaf eaten except for main veins and midrib	Gooseberry sawfly or Magpie moth
Leaves pale, bronze coloured, fall prematurely; fruits small, unappetizing	Gooseberry red spider mite
Dormant buds pecked out	Birds
Leaves covered with tiny pin pricks, distorted, tattered, brown; fruits mis-shapen and discoloured	Capsids
New shoots stunted, distorted, weak sideshoots	Greenfly
Sudden death of whole branch or branches, leaves brown and withered, fruit drop off	Die back
White powdery patches on young leaves and stems, later turning brown; fruits small, unpleasant looking	American gooseberry mildew
Bright red or orange patches on leaves and stems, fruit; later cup-like growths on patches	Cluster cup rust
Small, black-dotted spots; leaves yellow, fall prematurely	Leaf spot
Leaf edges curl up, look scorched, rest of leaf green	Potash deficiency

young stems; later the fruits are infected, and at a later stage the patches of fungus turn brown and can be peeled off like thin felt. Infected berries remain small; infected shoots are stunted and twisted.

Bushes grown in the open, and well pruned so that air can circulate freely around them, are less likely to be infected. As with die back, avoid using too much nitrogenous fertilizer which encourages weak sappy growth. If the infection is mild, cut off and burn infected shoots in spring as soon as seen. Any infection still appearing in summer should be cut off in late summer, no later, otherwise new growth may appear, which would not ripen before winter. If your bushes have suffered attacks of American gooseberry mildew in previous summers, a good preventive measure is to spray the bushes with dinocap or a mixture of washing soda and soft soap solution at the rate of 1 kg of washing soda and $\frac{1}{4}$ kg of soft soap mixed with 45 L of soft water (2 lb washing soda and $\frac{1}{2}$ lb soft soap mixed with 10 gal water). If the water is hard, double the quantity of soft soap. Spray before the flowers open, again as the fruit is setting and thereafter at 2-week intervals until it is controlled.

Cluster cup rust: this is another fungal disease likely to occur where bushes are grown in crowded or damp conditions. The main symptom is bright red or orange patches on the leaves, stems and fruits. Late in the summer, tiny cup-like growths develop on these red patches. All infected leaves, fruits and shoots should be burned. If your bushes have been infected with cluster cup rust before, spray them with Bordeaux mixture two weeks before flowering.

Leaf spot: blackcurrants are more susceptible to this disease than goose-berries, although the latter are some-times infected. It is most likely to occur in wet summers or areas which have high rainfall. The main symptoms are small, black-dotted spots; if the infection is severe, there will be large numbers of spots, the leaves will turn yellow, and fall prematurely. Rake up and burn all fallen leaves and remove infected leaves from the bushes. If the attack is severe, spray with zineb after removing the infected leaves, and again a fortnight later, and follow the manufacturer's directions with regard to precautions.

Potash deficiency: if the leaf edges develop brown bands around them, curl under and look scorched, while the rest of the leaf remains green and the new growth is short, then the plant is suffering from a shortage of potash. A further symptom is small berries which remain unripe. Correct this by applying sulphate of potash at the rate of 30 g per sq m (1 oz per sq yd) immediately. Thereafter apply 22-30 g per sq m ($\frac{3}{4}$-1 oz per sq yd) annually in early spring.

Varieties

Early

Keepsake: dessert or cooking; fruit size depends on picking date; pale green, oval and hairy, excellent flavour if left to ripen; bush vigorous and spreading with early foliage which protects young fruitlets from frost; reliable cropper but prone to mildew and flowers liable to frost damage.

May Duke: dessert or cooking; fruit deep crimson when mature, medium size, smooth skin, roundish oval shape; flavour better when cooked green; upright bush of moderate vigour.

New Giant: dessert or cooking; fruits large, yellowish green, well flavoured; bush upright, vigorous but not rampant.

Whitesmith: dessert or cooking; fruit pale greenish yellow to amber, medium to large, downy; bush upright, moderately vigorous; bush will spread with age.

Mid-season

Careless: cooking; fruits whitish-yellow, downy, large oval shape, veins sharply marked; bush moderately vigorous, spreading with age; resistent to mildew but does not do well under trees, or in poor soil, needs potash.

Lancashire Lad: cooking; fruit deep red, large if not overcropped, oval, hairy, moderate flavour; best picked green for cooking; bush vigorous and spreading, but needs good soil to do well; heavy cropper; *Lancashire Lad* is resistant to mildew.

Leveller: dessert or cooking; fruit large, oval, smooth, yellow-green veins sharply marked; good flavour, very popular variety; prolific cropper, but needs good soil conditions to do well; bush spreading; sulphur shy. Main commercial dessert variety.

Whinham's Industry: dessert or cooking; fruits large, hairy, oval and sweet, ripening dark red; upright vigorous growth later spreading; prolific cropper but subject to mildew; does well in semi-shade and under trees; may get too woody on rich soils; needs careful pruning for best results.

Langley Gage: dessert; fruit small, oval, pale greenish white, smooth, transparent with very sweet flavour; bush upright and vigorous.

Laxton's Amber; dessert or cooking; fruits yellow, medium-sized; bush upright in habit.

Late

Lancer (Howard's Lancer): dessert or cooking; fruit large, smooth, oval, very downy, greenish yellow; strong, vigorous growth and heavy cropper; grows well on most soils.

King of Trumps: dessert or cooking; fruits pale green; bush spreading but moderate growth; one of the latest of the late varieties.

Green Gem: dessert or cooking; fruits dark green with pale veins, medium to large, roundish oval; bush upright and compact; good and reliable cropper, resistant to mildew; worthwhile variety to grow but is often quite difficult to obtain.

White Lion: dessert or cooking; fruits white, large, oval, slightly hairy; growth vigorous and erect; best white variety for picking green and for dessert; very good flavour

Careless

Pears

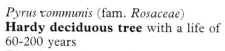

Pyrus communis (fam. *Rosaceae*)
Hardy deciduous tree with a life of
60-200 years
Planting to harvesting time: 5 years
Size: varies according to variety,
rootstock and training, but standard on
quince rootstock 3.6 m (12 ′) high, 2.7 m (9 ′) wide.
Yield: mature bush tree 25 kg (60 lb) fruit, dwarf pyramid
7 kg (15 lb), espalier 12 kg (25 lb)

One of the most delectable tree fruits, the best pears are home grown. This is because, like tomatoes, pears grown commercially must be tough-skinned to travel well without bruising, and remain firm fleshed for a relatively long period of time. The popular commercial varieties, such as *Williams* and *Conference*, are most often seen in shops because they meet these requirements, and not because they are particularly tasty. There are numerous dessert varieties which have sweeter, juicier and more succulent flesh; these are rarely seen in the markets because they are more easily bruised and are at their best for a short time only. These varieties, when picked fully ripe and warm from the sun, are a real luxury, and one which is available only to the home grower.

Pear trees used to have the reputation of being slow to crop; the old saying, "Plant pears for your heirs", was often quoted. Although this was true when pears were grown on pear rootstock, it no longer applies. Today pear trees are commonly grafted onto quince rootstock which makes them come into crop much

earlier. In one sense, however, the old saying still applies: pear trees are very long lived, and a healthy specimen may live for two hundred years or more. You can often see ancient pear trees in country gardens, still producing good-sized crops.

Another drawback which has largely been corrected is the problem of size. Wild pear trees (*Pyrus communis*), found in hedgerows and copses over much of Europe, are large trees, growing 15 m (50 ′) or more in height. Cultivated pears are descended from *Pyrus communis* and, like them, make lofty trees, much too large to prune, spray and harvest easily, and much too large for today's smaller gardens. Growing pears on quince rootstock has a considerable dwarfing effect, and bush, cordon, pyramid and espalier trained trees can easily be accommodated in a small garden.

Pears grown commercially are mostly open centred bushes, and this is probably the best method for the amateur and gives the highest yield in suitable conditions. However, most pears can be trained very easily and there are many other forms available. The dwarf pyramid, or central leader tree, follows the natural shape of the pear, which is upright; it is space saving and convenient for picking. In cool areas, or where shelter is required, it is worthwhile training an espalier against a wall.

Besides producing delicious crops, pear trees make very attractive features in the garden. In early to mid-spring they are covered with masses of white blossom, followed by leaves with a silvery sheen. The foliage of many varieties gives a rich display of autumn colour.

Pears can be divided into three groups according to use. Cooking pears are hard textured, and less juicy and flavourful than dessert varieties; slow cooking with plenty of sugar improves them. They are prolific croppers, however, and tend to keep better than dessert varieties. In the north of England and in cool, exposed sites they are more likely to succeed.

The second category is made up of pears having a very high tannin content. These perry pears are very bitter and are not eaten. They are pressed for their juice, which is then fermented and made into perry, an alcoholic beverage. The varieties planted for perry are not usually available to the amateur grower, although there are commercial perry orchards in southwest England.

Lastly, and probably the best category for the amateur grower, are the dessert pears. These are softer in texture, and often have a sweet aroma. Dessert pears appreciate a warm, sheltered site; in cooler areas these varieties do best when trained as an espalier cordon, or fan, and grown against a wall. Dessert varieties will cook and bottle well if picked before they are slightly ripe; they are the best choice for the small garden.

Suitable site and soil
Because pears are Mediterranean in origin, they thrive in warmer conditions than apples. Pears are therefore more successfully grown in the south of England than the north. It is possible to grow dessert pears in cold areas if they are given wall protection; otherwise select a late cooking variety for growing in the open.

Pat Brindley

A Conference *pear tree trained as an espalier against a wall. Pears flower about a month earlier than apples, so they are more vulnerable to frost damage. Select a site which is warm, sunny, and fairly sheltered from winds, so insects can pollinate the flowers successfully.*

Pears blossom about four weeks earlier in the season than apples, so they are more vulnerable to damage from spring frosts. Avoid low-lying ground or frost pockets. Exposure to strong winds at flowering time can cause considerable damage, as well; insects are discouraged from visiting the blossom, and tender young leaves will be torn or even stripped off the tree. Autumnal winds can dessicate older leaves and cause premature fruit fall. Wind-bruised pear leaves always turn black. Try to site pear trees in as warm and sheltered a position as possible.

Pears will tolerate less well drained soil conditions than apples, but will not survive dry root conditions. The ideal soil for pears is a deep heavy loam which is slightly acid. Extremely alkaline soils may lead to chlorosis (yellowing) of the leaves. Whatever the soil type, there should be at least 60 cm (2 ') of rooting depth.

Buying a tree
There are several factors to consider when selecting a pear tree, or trees, if you have room for more than one. Choose wisely because the chances are you will be living with the tree for a long time. It is an expensive and time-consuming proposition to replace unsatisfactory trees with more suitable varieties two or three years later, and much time will be wasted unnecessarily.

There are many named varieties from which to choose; this is further complicated by the fact that these will be grafted on one of several possible rootstocks, each with its own growth pattern. Lastly, pears are available as maidens or in a variety of trained shapes: standards, half-standards, bushes, cordons, espaliers, pyramids and fans.

The main determining factor is the size of your garden; if it is fairly small select a self-pollinating variety, such as *Dr Jules Guyot* or *Marguerite Marillat* trained in bush or pyramid form. Although some pear varieties are self-fertile, most require a second variety to ensure fertilization, and even self-fertile varieties bear heavier crops when there is a suitable pear tree nearby. Some have exceptionally poor pollen, and need two different varieties for satisfactory fertilization, but fortunately there are not many of these. *Jargonelle* is one. For successful pollination, trees must flower at the same time; however, certain varieties will not cross-pollinate each other and' some varieties will not pollinate any others, so check with your local nurseryman.

Pears are either grafted onto quince or pear rootstocks. Malling Quince A is probably the most popular quince rootstock; it produces trees of moderate vigour and high fruit production. Quince C rootstock has a dwarfing effect, producing bushes rather than trees; ideal for the smaller garden. Pears on Quince C come into fruit earlier than on Quince A. Some popular varieties, such as *Williams bon Crétien*, do not unite properly with quince when grafted; they are said to be incompatible. These varieties are double grafted by the nursery, using an intervening compatible variety to prevent a future break at the union; this is why some varieties are more expensive to buy.

Pear rootstocks are used to make large standard trees of vigorous growth. These are not suitable for the small garden because they grow too big to prune and harvest easily; trees on pear rootstock also take much longer to come into crop.

Buy maidens or two or three-year-old trees, if possible. They will settle down more quickly than a four or five-year-old and you can train them exactly as you wish from the beginning.

Planting
Prepare the soil well in advance by breaking up the subsoil and incorporating plenty of well-rotted manure. Correct the pH level if it is below 6.0 by liming, allowing at least two months to elapse between manuring and liming. About two weeks before planting, work

In today's smaller gardens, pears grown as bushes, cordons, or pyramids make the most economical use of space. Besides luscious fruit, the flowers are most attractive, and some varieties have leaves which turn rich shades of crimson in the autumn.

Donald Smith

in a general compound fertilizer at the rate of 60 g per sq m (2 oz per sq yd).

Autumn-planted trees establish themselves quickest; try to plant them as soon as possible after leaf fall. If the soil is frozen or very wet, heel the trees in until conditions improve. Plant, stake, and mulch as for apple (see APPLE). Spread out the roots so they occupy the maximum amount of soil from which to draw water and nutrients.

Take care to keep the union of the scion and the rootstock at least 7.5 cm (3″) above soil level. If the scion roots, the named variety will quickly dominate the rootstock and an over-vigorous, unfruitful tree will result.

Bush trees should be spaced 3-3.7 m (10-12′) apart; pyramids can be as close as 1.8 m (6′). Pears growing against a wall should be allowed a minimum of 2.1m (8′) height and a spread of 3.6 m (12′).

Pruning an open-centred bush

The initial pruning to shape an open centred bush is the same as that for apples (see APPLE) with two important differences. Most varieties of pear, if correctly pruned, carry their fruit on spurs close to the main branches and therefore more main branches can be allowed for each tree, say twelve, where eight would be more suitable for apples. Secondly, pear branches in the young tree are naturally slender and have a tendency to droop. To counteract this, continue to prune the leading shoots on the main branches by one third to one half of the new growth, according to vigour, until the trees approach their allotted height and spread. This will be when they are about eight years old, when leader pruning should cease.

Leaders are pruned back for four reasons: to strengthen the branch, to encourage more side growth, to remove deformed or diseased wood and to remove a branch growing in an undesirable direction. If none of these apply, then leader pruning should cease.

Some pears are tip-bearers, which means that instead of producing fruit on

PYRAMID PRUNING

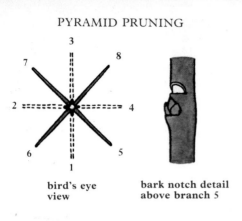

bird's eye
view

bark notch detail
above branch 5

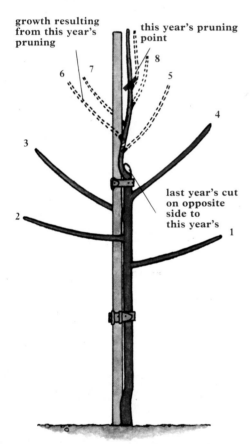

growth resulting
from this year's
pruning

this year's pruning
point

last year's cut
on opposite
side to
this year's

*Prune central leader each winter to
encourage new tier of branches to form. Cut
to a bud pointing in the opposite direction of
the previous year's bud; leave about 20 cm
(8″) of new growth. Choose four well placed
buds to intersect existing branches. Stimulate
lowest bud to grow by notching bark over it.*

short spurs, these are formed on the end
of branches. *Josephine de Malines* and
Jargonelle are tip-bearers; they should be
pruned very lightly, and for this reason
are not really good for restricted
training. They are also better with a
longer trunk than is usual in bush forms,
up to as much as 30 cm (12″) longer.

Training and pruning a pyramid

Because most pear trees are upright in
growth, they are very suitable for
training as pyramids. Pyramids grow
with a strong central leader, and are
similar in form to a Christmas tree. From
this central trunk cropping branches
grow away at wide angles with about 30
cm (1′) of trunk between each tier of
branches. The resulting tree is a very
compact and efficient fruit bearer.
Formative pruning is done in winter;
pruning to encourage fruiting and
restrictive growth is done in summer.

To train a pyramid pear tree, buy a
maiden or two-year-old. Cut the tree
back to about 50 cm (20″) the first winter
it is in your garden, making the cut
immediately above a conveniently
placed bud. Rub out the first bud below
the leader bud. Make sure there are three
or four buds left, spaced evenly around
and down the stem. These will grow out
to form the first tier of framework
branches. The lowest bud should ensure
that there is a leg of about 23-30 cm (9-
12″). Any 'feathers' should be cut off
flush with the main stem. The following
winter, and each subsequent winter until
the desired height is reached, prune the
leader, leaving 20 cm (8″) of new growth;
cut to a bud pointing in the opposite
direction to the previous year's bud.
This keeps the leader growing straight.
Make sure there are three well-placed
buds on the remaining part of the leader
to make additional whorls of branches.
These buds should be as evenly spaced
round and down the stem as possible;
ideally they should point towards the
gaps between branches on the tier below.

Do not retain a bud immediately
above an existing branch, but aim for

even spacing both up and around. Rub out all unwanted buds; this can be done by pushing them off with your thumb.

The branches and sideshoots are pruned in summer. Start when the new growth has begun to mature and the shoots are becoming stiff and woody, and brown at the base. Disregarding the cluster of leaves at the base of the new growth, count five or six leaves along the branches and cut beyond a downward pointing one. While the tree is still young flowers may form on the central leader; these should be removed to encourage the production of more side branches.

From late mid-summer, when the sideshoots along the branches begin to mature and are about 30 cm (1´) long and woody at the base, cut to the second or third leaf beyond the basal cluster. This helps to build up strong spurs, close to the main branches. Where there has been growth from a sideshoot pruned in previous years, prune back to the first leaf beyond the basal cluster. Spread out the work over a period of three to four weeks. If in winter you find there has been further growth from any of these summer cuts, prune it back to the first bud.

Restrict the final height of the pyramid to about 2.1 m (7´), by switching pruning from winter to late spring, just after new growth has begun. Cut the central leader back to within 1.2 cm ($\frac{1}{2}$″) of its new growth. When branch leaders reach the length of those in the tier below, or begin to grow close to branches of adjacent trees, deal with them in the same way, by cutting them back.

Training an espalier

Espaliers can be trained against walls, fences or specially erected posts and wires. An espalier tree has a strong central leader from which branch out horizontal pairs of opposite laterals, each tier parallel to the others. Nurseries usually sell two and three tier espaliers, but these are expensive and if you train

your own, you can make it fit exactly into the available space.

Espaliers need wires, whether against walls or in the open, 30 cm (1´) from the ground, and additional wires for each tier at intervals of about 30 cm (1´). A horizontal space of 4.2 m (14´) is best.

To train your own espalier, buy a maiden or two-year-old. Immediately after planting, cut the leader back to a strong bud, about 5 cm (2″) higher than the lowest wire. This bud will produce a vertical shoot. Below this top bud, select two buds, on opposite sides of the stem; these will eventually become the laterals forming the first tier. Notch above the lower bud. Rub out any other buds.

During the first summer, tie the middle shoot to a cane with soft string; attach the cane vertically to the wires. When they become long enough, attach the shoots from the two lower buds to canes as well. Fasten the canes to the wires at an angle of 45°, so that the two lower shoots will be at a 90° angle from each other. Try to keep the two growing equally strongly so they are the same length. If they are growing unequally, lower the cane of the stronger shoot to impede the flow of sap and thus slow it down; raise the cane of the other slightly to encourage growth.

In late autumn or winter, unfasten the two side canes and bring the branches down to the horizontal wires; secure the branches to the bottom wire. However, if they have to be forced down to the horizontal, it is better to leave them and continue to lower them the following summer, finally tying them in when they are two years old, in their second winter. In winter, prune the vertical leader to a strong bud about 5 cm (2″) above the second wire. Proceed as in the first winter, choosing two more buds to fill the second wire. Continue in this way until the required number of tiers has been formed. When forming the final tier, allow only two shoots to form, one on either side of the central leader, and cut the leading growth back to about 2.5 cm (1″) above the highest of the two sideshoots. Prune established espalier branches in summer. Prune the side growths as they mature to the third leaf beyond the basal cluster. Cut shoots from laterals that were pruned previously to one leaf beyond the basal cluster at the twig base (see diagram). When the main branches of each tier have filled the space available, cut them back in late spring as required.

Fertilizers and care
During the first winter, check the trees after hard ground frost and firm any which have lifted. Pears, particularly

young trees, are very sensitive to water shortage. In dry weather, water thoroughly. Watering in late spring or early summer tends to encourage shoot growth, while watering in mid- and late summer aids in fruit swelling. Trees planted against walls are particularly vulnerable to drought, as soil near foundations dries out very quickly.

Pears respond more than any other fruit tree to applications of bulky organic matter. For the the first three springs after planting, give an annual mulch of well-rotted manure, 5 cm (2") thick in late spring; spread it over an area

TRAINING AN ESPALIER

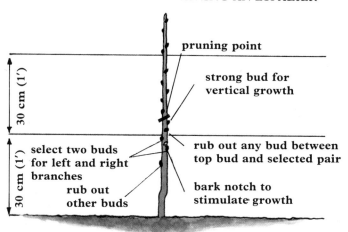

pruning point

strong bud for vertical growth

30 cm (1')

select two buds for left and right branches
rub out other buds

30 cm (1')

rub out any bud between top bud and selected pair

bark notch to stimulate growth

1. Espaliers need wire supports, whether in the open or against walls, 30 cm (1') from the ground, and at 30 cm (1') intervals. Immediately after planting, cut the leader back to a strong bud 5 cm (2") higher than the lowest wire. Select two opposite buds to form laterals, notch the lower one, and rub out the rest.

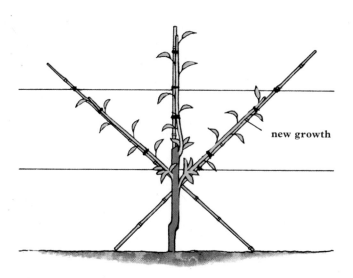

new growth

2. The first summer, tie middle shoot to a cane with soft string; when they grow long enough, tie the lateral shoots to canes as well. The middle cane should be vertical, and the two lateral canes at an angle of 45° from the ground. If the sideshoots grow unequally, lower the cane of the stronger shoot to slow it down; raise the cane of the other slightly

equivalent to that covered by the tree's branches. Keep the manure at least 15 cm (6″) away from the trunk. Supplement this with an annual dressing of 30 g (1 oz) sulphate of ammonia and 15 g ($\frac{1}{2}$ oz) of sulphate of potash per sq m (sq yd) applied in late winter or early spring.

Pears are very nitrogen greedy; for this reason they should not be grassed down. There is one exception, however. If you wish to retard the growth of over-vigorous cordons or dwarf pyramids, then grassing down is a good method. Trees competing with grass for moisture and nutrients will be slower than those in cultivated ground.

Spur and fruit thinning
Pears make spurs more readily than apples and as the tree gets older the spurs may become crowded. When this happens, spur pruning is beneficial; prune the oldest and least fruitful ones back to their base. Any spurs which are too long can be shortened by about half. All spur pruning is best done in winter.

Pears tend to produce a great deal of

3. In autumn, undo the two side canes and bring the branches down to the horizontal wires; secure the branches to the bottom wire. In the second autumn, the same procedure is followed to produce a second tier, and again until the top tier has filled the top wire.

PRUNING ESPALIER LATERALS

pruning point one leaf above basal cluster on sub-side-shoot

pruning point three leaves above basal cluster on side-shoot

basal cluster of leaves

Prune espaliers in mid-summer. Cut mature laterals growing from horizontal branches to three leaves above basal cluster; cut sideshoots back to one leaf above.

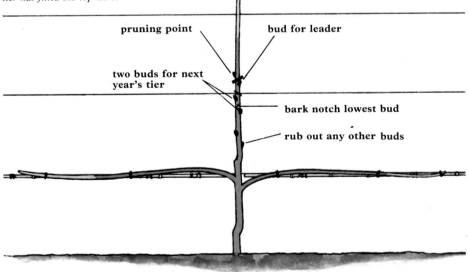

pruning point

bud for leader

two buds for next year's tier

bark notch lowest bud

rub out any other buds

SPUR PRUNING ON OLD TREES

Pear fruiting spurs will become overcrowded in time, and fruit production may diminish. When this happens, cut out the oldest and least fruitful spurs back to their base with secateurs or a sharp pruning knife in winter.

blossom; if all was allowed to produce fruit it would exhaust the tree. Judicious fruit thinning is usually necessary although pears need less thinning than apples. Thin first in late spring, when the young fruitlets are about 2.5 cm (1″) long. Remove and burn all mis-shapen ones first, as they probably contain pear midge larvae. A second thinning, after the natural fruit fall in early summer, should be done in mid-summer. There should be a final spacing of 12.5 cm (5″) between fruit. This varies slightly according to the age, health and variety of the tree; vigorous mature trees can carry heavier crops than very young or weak-growing ones.

Harvesting

Pears, more so than apples, need to be picked and eaten at exactly the right moment, as most varieties are at their best for a short while only. Very early varieties, which are ready mid- to late summer, can be picked straight off the tree and eaten at once. As soon as the base skin colour begins to yellow or pale, is about the right stage. Early varieties, like *Williams Bon Chrétien*, should be picked before they are fully ripe.

This will mean picking them when the skin at the stalk end of the fruit starts to change colour. If left on the tree for longer, they will become too mature, and although the outside may appear just right, the centre will have started to rot.

Mid-season varieties, ie early to mid-autumn kinds, are picked, and then kept in a cool place for about a week or so before eating. To tell if a pear is ripe, lift the fruit and twist it slightly; ripe pears should part quite easily from the tree. If pears are picked too soon for storing, they will become 'sleepy', when the outer flesh becomes soft but does not develop its flavour, and the inner remains hard. The best criterion for picking for store is the ground colour of the skin; when this begins to change, the fruit can be picked. When harvesting, handle the pears carefully as they bruise easily, particularly at the stalk end. Try to pick the fruit in dry weather, as pears rapidly deteriorate if left wet for any length of time.

Storing

Unfortunately, pears do not keep as well as apples, so if you want a steady supply, it it best to plant several varieties of trees with fruit which ripen in succession. Early and mid-season varieties do not keep for any length of time; it is not worth arranging long-term storage, as you will more than likely be disappointed. Late varieties need to be picked when slightly unripe and stored until they reach their full flavour. If a sharp tug is needed to get the fruit off, they are not ready for storing. Leave them for a couple of days and try again. Be guided also by the change in the ground colour,

1. To get healthy, good sized pears, thin fruit in late spring and mid-summer; remove mis-shapen fruit.

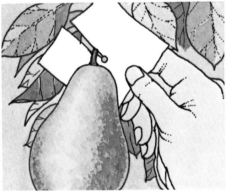

2. Ripening pears are vulnerable to attacks by birds; protect the fruit by fixing cardboard squares onto stalks.

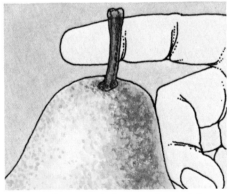

3. If picking pears for storing, pick fruit with the stalk intact, otherwise the pears are liable to rot.

especially near the stalk end; when this begins to change, the fruit is ready for storing. Pick the fruit when dry, with the stalk intact. Store only sound, un-blemished fruit; any damaged pears will quickly rot and the rot will spread.

Do not wrap them, but lay them in a single layer on slatted trays in cool 4-7 C (40-45 F) conditions. An empty room or shed will do, as long as there are no severe fluctuations in temperature. They are better in some humidity, and shrivel quickly in a dry store. Inspect them frequently for approaching maturity, which is indicated by a softening of the flesh close to the stalk. Then bring them into a warm room for a couple of days, to finish off the ripening process.

Exhibition tips
Pears for exhibition are divided into two categories: cooking and dessert. The methods of preparation and presentation are the same for both. In both categories the judges will look for large fruits with eyes and stalks intact. The skins should be clear and unblemished, and the colour appropriate to the variety. Six is the usual number shown of the same variety, and they should be as uniform as possible. Do not include one or two enormous pears, which would make the remaining fruit seem small by com-parison, and spoil the exhibit. Never display over-ripe pears, small, mis-shapen fruits, or fruits with blemishes.

To get the best pears, thin the crop while the fruits are still small. As the selected pears ripen, expose them gradually to more and more sunshine, by carefully removing the leaves closest to them and tying back the overhanging foliage. Pick more pears than the actual number needed, so that you have a reserve supply when you are setting up the exhibit.

Pears shaped like apples are usually staged with eyes uppermost, and stalk end downwards; place one fruit in the centre and the remaining fruit around it. You can raise the central fruit slightly by placing white tissue paper underneath it.

Varieties

Although *Conference* and *William's Bon Chrétien* are the most popular, there are many other fine flavoured varieties which should be planted more often. Remember that the more varieties you plant, the better crops you will have from each.

Summer pears

Beurré Bedford: large, pale yellow fruit, relatively resistant to scab; fruit ripens late summer or early autumn; erect and compact growth; mid-season flowering.

Doyenné d'Été: small, yellow, conical fruit; one of the first to ripen in mid to late summer; juicy and pleasant flavour; tree has weak but spreading growth; flowers early to mid-season; not very good for restricted training.

Jargonelle: very old variety but still popular; long, greenish-yellow, tapering fruit; relatively scab resistant; heavy cropper; will do well in the north of England or on north-facing wall; flowers mid-season; tree large, spreading growth, tip-bearing; must have two pollinators, *Beurré Superfin* is suitable.

Early to mid-autumn pears

Gorham: long, pale yellow pear with heavy russeting; good flavour; fills the gap between *William's* and *Conference*; scab resistant; tree of hardy and upright growth; late flowering.

Dr Jules Guyot: self-fertile variety; better flavour than *Conference*; yellow fruit, black dotted skin, often flushed scarlet; tree fertile and hardy, upright growth; flowers late in season.

Fertility Improved: sweet, juicy, crisp pear; heavy cropper, often needs thinning; disease resistant; self-fertile; fruit small, yellow, but heavily russeted; tree tall and upright in growth with red autumn foliage; flowers late in season.

Marguerite Marillat: self-fertile pear, although it will not pollinate other varieties; crops well; yellow flesh, skin flushed with bright scarlet; upright, small tree with scarlet autumn leaves; flowers early, so avoid a frost pocket.

William's Bon Chrétien: best known and most widely grown of all pears, also called *Bartlett*; irregular, roundish, pale yellow fruit with red flush; moderate flavour, juicy flesh; very susceptible to scab; upright tree, suitable for training against north wall; needs double working; flowers mid-season.

Merton Pride: green pear of good size; very good flavour; heavy cropper; tree upright in growth; flowers mid-season.

Mid to late autumn pears

Beurré Hardy: large, round, conical, coppery russeted fruit with red flush; very good flavour; fertile; relatively resistant to scab; tree vigorous, full and spreading; prune lightly; leaves scarlet in autumn; flowers late in season; fruits best picked a little before they part readily from the tree; keep two or three weeks before eating.

Beurré Superfin: long, golden yellow fruit patched with russet; less vigorous pear good for small gardens; makes good cordons; fruit does not keep well, pick late in early autumn; mid-season flowering.

Conference: most reliable of all pears; long, pale green fruit with silvery russet; prolific cropper; pick late in early autumn and keep one to three weeks before eating; self-fertile but will do better if cross-pollinated; vulnerable to wind damage and scab; moderate flavour; flowers mid-season.

Doyenné du Comice: large, roundish, golden fruit with light russetting and red flush; superb flavour; not entirely reliable in bad years or bad locations; needs several varieties to pollinate, to ensure regularly good crops; very susceptible to scab and sulphur-shy; vigorous upright growth; good against wall or as cordon; flowers late in season; pick late in early autumn or early in mid-autumn and keep a few weeks.

Louise Bonne of Jersey: greenish-yellow fruit, flushed red; flesh white and delicious; fertile; tree hardy and vigorous; upright in growth; regular cropper; exceptionally beautiful blossom; flowers early in the season.

Durondeau: fruits long, tapering, red russet; good flavour; stores well; tree small, suitable for small gardens; spurs well and is good in restricted forms; red autumn foliage; crops heavily in suitable soil; flowers mid-season.

Packham's Triumph: fruits broad, squat, bright green changing to bright yellow; juicy, very sweet; crops well, and ripens 10 days before *Comice*; moderate sized, tip-bearing tree; flowers mid-season.

Early and mid-winter pears

Glou Morceau: green pears, turning yellow when ripe; sweet flavour, keeps well; does best on sunny wall or in sheltered garden; flowers late in season.

Joséphine de Malines: small, green fruit, yellow when ripe with a russet patch; flesh pink, with delicious scent and sweet flavour; best of all winter pears; stores well; fruit ripens unevenly in store, so inspect regularly; fertile and reliable cropper, especially in warm gardens; tip-bearing and tending to droop; flowers mid-season.

Winter Nelis: juicy, sweet, smallish pear, best eaten while still yellowish green; fertility good and useful for pollinating *Comice*; ripens over a month or more; tree has slender, arching growth; scab resistant; flowers late in season.

Santa Claus: excellent type to choose if growing on a sheltered wall; may not be successful in harsh climates; heavy cropper of well-flavoured brownish-red russet fruits; vigorous, upright growth; very attractive in autumn when foliage turns crimson and purple.

Late cooking pears

Catillac: large, green, cooking pear remaining hard until mid-spring; scab resistant; tree spreading with broad leaves and large flowers; vigorous cropper but needs two other trees to pollinate it; blossoms late in season.

Pests & Diseases

Pears suffer from the same trouble as apples, but generally to a lesser degree. Natural predators and good cultivation, including regular feeding, should reduce the risk of damage considerably. If you have had serious trouble in the past, an annual spraying programme should be carried out, to control the damage done by a particular pest or disease, otherwise follow a system of 'spot' spraying. A tar oil wash applied in mid to late winter will control the eggs of aphids and leaf suckers, but is best applied only once every three or four years, as it also kills many beneficial insect predators. In early spring, at the green cluster stage, spray with captan against scab. In mid-spring, at the early white bud stage, spray with malathion to control aphids, caterpillars and pear midge and apply captan again for scab. Lastly, in mid to late spring, at petal fall when nearly all the blossom is off, apply captan against scab. Never spray fully open flowers, because of the danger to bees and other pollinating insects. Not all pesticides and fungicides are compatible, so follow manufacturer's instructions before applying them together. And remember that these substances can also be dangerous to pets and children, so be sure they are properly stored.

Aphids: these sometimes infest young growth, causing the leaves and shoot tips to curl and the new shoots to be stunted, sometimes severely. The leaves may also become sticky. The insects are small, green, grey or dark brown in colour, and are usually found on the underside of the leaves. The most serious is the pear bedstraw species, which is a mealy-covered, pink aphid; in severe attacks the whole tree may be smothered. Remove and destroy aphid-infested shoots as soon as they appear and spray the tree with derris or malathion; the winter tar-oil wash will kill most of the overwintering eggs.

Pear sucker: in recent years this has been causing a good deal of trouble. It is a small, flat, pale green, sucking insect which feeds on the undersides of the leaves, and the flower trusses, in bud and open. Three generations can occur in a season. Leaves have pale green patches on them, flowers do not develop, and sticky 'honeydew' with black mould on it, covers the leaves and shoots. The winter tar-oil wash will deal with the eggs, or derris or malathion can be used in spring.

Pear midge: if the young fruitlets on your tree do not develop, but become badly mis-shapen, turn black and fall off the tree, then pear midge is the probable cause. The tiny, white maggots, 3-4 mm $\frac{1}{8}-\frac{1}{6}''$) long, live in the young fruit, and later move to the soil where they overwinter.

Thorough cultivation under the trees will expose the maggots to insect-eating birds, the weather and physical damage from hoeing. Remove and burn all infested fruitlets, before the larvae have a chance to get to the soil. If this pest has caused considerable damage in the past, spray with gamma HCH at the white bud stage, but not during flowering.

Pear leaf blister mite: this microscopic insect spends winters beneath the bud scales and during the summer lives inside the leaves. Infested leaves will have numerous yellowish green or reddish pustules on them, from mid-spring onwards. The pustules eventually turn brown to black by mid-summer, and the leaves fall early. If the attack is a mild one, pick off and burn all infested leaves. In general, this is usually all that is needed in the private garden. However, if you have had serious trouble in the past, spray with lime sulphur in early spring as the buds start to open. Do not spray *Doyenne du Comice* with lime sulphur, as it is sulphur shy.

Caterpillars: there are several varieties of caterpillar which may attack pear trees, including the fruit tree tortrix moth, the vapourer, lackey and winter moths. The treatment is the same for all types of caterpillars: hand-pick the caterpillars in the case of mild infestations, or spray with trichlorphon in severe attacks.

Fireblight: this is a very serious bacterial infection which enters the tree through the flowers, and moves from the spurs into the main branches. Dieback occurs and leaves turn brown and black but remain on the tree. It is seen mostly on new shoots which look as though they have been scorched by flame. Cankers develop beneath infected tissues, which ooze a sticky liquid in spring. This liquid contains bacteria, which are then carried by rain or insects to other trees.

If you suspect fireblight, you must notify your local representative of the Ministry of Agriculture, who will then give you instructions about treatment.

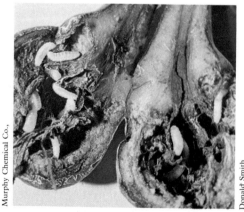

This fruit is infested with pear midge larvae; control with gamma HCH spray in spring.

Pear leaf blister mite infestation: the minute insects live in the leaves and destroy them.

Pear scab: this fungal infection appears as blackish scabs on the fruit, or dark brown blotches on the leaves. Occasionally shoots are infected and they will appear blistery and scabby. Remove and destroy all diseased leaves; do not leave them on the ground, or the infection will spread rapidly. Spray with captan (except for fruit to be preserved) as indicated. For fruit for preserving, use benomyl at bud burst, and at three-weekly intervals as long as necessary. In winter, be very careful to prune off all infested shoots, as the spores overwinter on them and can remain viable for at least three years. The scab lesions also provide a means of entry for the fungus disease canker.

Pear stony pit virus: if the pears are mis-shaped and pitted, and have small, hard areas in the flesh, then the tree is infected with stony pit virus. In severe cases, the fruit will be completely inedible. At first, fruit on single branches will be affected, but eventually the virus spreads through the whole tree, and the whole harvest from that tree becomes useless. Old trees are most susceptible. There is no cure; dig up and burn any infected tree.

Canker: this fungus disease also attacks apple trees, and the symptoms and damage are the same. The bark of branches becomes sunken and cracked; if the canker girdles a stem, it will die above the infection. Cut out all infected parts and paint large wounds with a tree wound-sealing compound.

Pear scab: this is a fungal infection which attacks leaves and shoots as well as fruit.

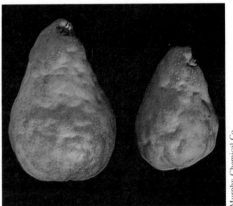

Murphy Chemical Co.

Pears having stony pit virus are mis-shapen and inedible; old trees are most vulnerable.

GUIDE TO PEAR TROUBLES

Symptom	Probable Cause
Leaves sticky and curled, shoots curled	Aphids
Pale green patches and sticky honeydew on leaves, flowers do not develop	Pear sucker
Mis-shapen black fruitlets	Pear midge
Pale green or red pustules on leaves	Pear leaf blister mite
Leaves eaten	Caterpillars
Leaves turn brown or black and remain on tree, oozing cankers on branches and trunk	Fireblight
Dark brown blotches on leaves, blackish scabs on fruit	Pear scab
Fruit mis-shapen and pitted, with small hard areas in the flesh	Pear stony pit virus

Plums

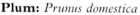

Plum: *Prunus domestica*
(fam. *Rosaceae*)
Damson: *Prunus damascena*
Gage: *Prunus italica*
Bullace: *Prunus insititia*

Hardy deciduous tree with a useful life of 50 years
Planting to harvesting time: 4-5 years
Size: 6-9 m (20-30′) tall; less on trained shapes
Yield: mature standard or bush tree on St. Julien A
rootstock 22-26 kg (50-60 lb), more for a more vigorous
rootstock, less for a pyramid tree. Greengages yield half this
figure.

Plums are among the most delicious and succulent tree fruits, and a freshly picked plum is one of summer's finest treats. The trees are hardier and easier to grow than peaches and cherries, and they will succeed in nearly all types of soil.

Damsons, gages and bullaces are all closely related to plums and their cultivation is basically similar.

Plums are usually divided into cooking and dessert varieties. Cooking plums are mainly dark coloured, with blue-black skins, and have less flesh and a tarter flavour than the dessert varieties. The trees which produce cooking plums are usually larger, hardier and more reliable croppers than the dessert varieties. Dessert plums have a richer flavour, higher sugar content, and may be yellow, green, red, blue-black, or purple-skinned. Most dessert plums are partly descended from the gages and, like the gages, do best in sunny sheltered

conditions, trained against a wall.

Bullace is a species of cooking plum which is sometimes found growing wild in hedgerows and woodlands. Bullace is very similar to the sloe, or blackthorn, and forms a small, hardy, ornamental tree. It is a useful shelter tree, and is sometimes planted in rows along the edge of an orchard. The fruit is very sharp-flavoured, and is usually left on the tree until late autumn, so that frosts can soften the acidity. Bullaces are not eaten raw, but are excellent for preserving and jam-making.

Damson is another cooking variety closely related to the bullace, and is also found growing wild in hedgerows. The trees produce oval fruit in early to mid-autumn, which are smaller and sweeter flavoured than those of the bullace. The fruits are cooked when ripe and are used for tarts, jam-making and bottling. They are very tough trees, and will crop well

A fan-trained plum, newly planted against a wall. All but north-facing sites are suitable.

even on thin soil. Damsons flower later than other plums, and are less damaged by frosts and cold winds. They also keep their leaves late into autumn and like the bullace can be used as windbreaks for less hardy trees.

Closely related to the bullaces and damsons are the gages which are used mainly as dessert plums. These are usually green-fleshed, with green, occasionally red-flushed, skin. Greengages may also be yellow-skinned and yellow-fleshed. Regardless of the colour, they are generally considered to be the sweetest and most deliciously scented of the plums. Unfortunately, gages need more favourable growing conditions

than other plums, and are best grown as a fan-trained tree against a south-facing wall.

Suitable site and soil

Because there are no really effective dwarfing rootstocks, plums eventually make large trees. They are unsuitable for small gardens unless they are fan-trained, or grown as a pyramid or bush. Plums can be grown as standards or half-standards if you have a large garden.

Remembering that you need to plan for the size of a mature tree, you should expect the following heights from the different shapes: fans 2 m (7′); pyramids 2.4 m (8′); half-standards and standards

A lovely crop of golden plums. Three-year-old purchased fans should start fruiting in two years.

Pat Brindley

6-9 m (20-30'); bushes 3.5-4.5 m (12-15').

Plums start to flower earlier than most other fruit trees, in mid-spring, so if your garden is in a low-lying area or subject to frosts, it is best to choose a late-flowering variety, and give it wall protection. Although plums do best in full sunshine, they can crop well with less light than pears need. If there is protection from frost, some varieties of plums can be grown against east or west walls, leaving the southerly positions for pears or peaches.

Because plums need a lot of moisture in the soil, do not plant them next to large trees, particularly those which are surface-rooting, like elms. Annual rainfall should ideally be between 50 and 76 cm (20-30"). Although plums need a continual supply of moisture at the roots, the subsoil must never be stagnant or badly drained. A heavy loam or clay soil is preferable, and one that is neither very acid nor very alkaline. Although the trees crop better when some lime is added to the soil, they do not need an enormous amount, and on chalky soils the trees may show symptoms of iron deficiency.

Buying a tree

Because there are so many varieties and shapes available, there are several factors

60

to consider before making your purchase. A major consideration is the ultimate size; this is controlled to a large extent by the rootstock. A few varieties are grown on their own roots, but most plums are budded or grafted onto other rootstocks of known performance. Myrobalan B rootstock will give a large tree, too vigorous for the small garden. St. Julian A rootstock is semi-dwarfing and is more suitable for the small garden. Brompton rootstock is also good for the small garden, as trees grafted onto it will grow steadily and come in to bearing quickly, and Brompton rootstock sends up very few suckers. The common plum rootstock is also semi-dwarfing, and is often used as a rootstock for gages.

The grafting of named varieties onto rootstocks is complicated by the fact that not all varieties are compatible with all rootstocks. If an unsuitable combination is made between the scion, or shoot of the named variety, and rootstock, the tree may break where the two join together. A good nurseryman will choose a suitable rootstock according to the variety, shape and size of the tree to be grown. Make sure you buy your trees from a reputable source.

Size is also controlled, to a lesser extent, by the way the tree is trained. You can either buy a ready trained standard, half-standard, or bush tree; these are either two or three years old. Alternatively, you can buy a one-year-old maiden, and train it yourself.

Pollination

A second point to consider when buying a tree is pollination. A few plums, such as *Victoria,* are self-fertile, but most require a compatible pollinator which flowers at the same time, and even the self-fertile varieties will set heavier crops if cross-pollinated. Timing the cross-pollination is less difficult than with apples and pears, because flowering of all plum varieties takes place within the space of 18 or 19 days; from early spring onwards. Plums are divided into 'early' and 'late' flowering for pollination

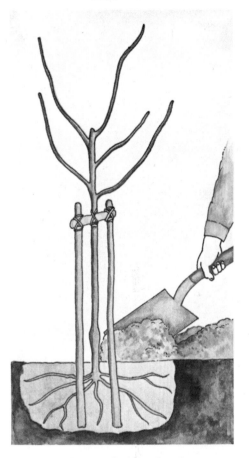

1. **Allow plenty of room for the roots. Stake the tree for support. Return soil, making sure it penetrates between roots. Press down very firmly.**

purposes. Unless they have been damaged by frost, the trees will remain in flower for exactly 10 days, so the early trees will have just about finished flowering when the late flowering varieties are starting to bloom. Early self-fertile varieties will pollinate early self-sterile varieties, and the same is true for those varieties which bloom later. If you have room in your garden for only one tree, choose a self-fertile one. If you are buying more than one tree, check the Varieties list for suitable pollinators.

If you plan to grow gages, remember that they tend to produce rather small

61

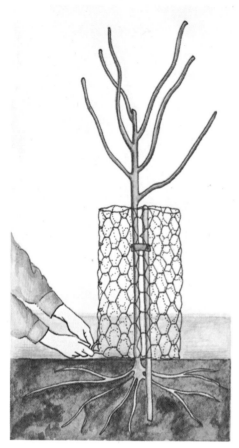

2. If rabbits or other animal pests are likely to be a problem, protect the newly planted tree with wire netting. Leave no gaps at the base.

3. An alternative staking method: make sure the pole is not so long as to interfere with growing branches. Use a soft, strong material to tie.

crops. Hence it is a good idea to plant two trees, either two varieties of gages or a gage and another plum tree.

Planting out

This is best done in late autumn, but an open-grown tree can be planted from late autumn to early spring, provided the weather is suitable. If your soil is heavy, you should work in coarse sand before planting, at the rate of 3 kg per sq m (7 lb per sq yd). Make freely draining soil more water retentive by mixing in rotted organic matter, at the rate of 12 L per sq m (2½ gal per sq yd). This is particularly

important if you are planting the tree against a wall, as the soil near walls tends to be dry. In general, plums will not grow well on light, 'hot' soils.

Plant and stake the trees as for apples (see the relevant chapter on apples), making sure you firm well round the tree. Also, make sure the union between the rootstock and scion is at least 7.5 cm (3″) above ground level, or the scion will form its own roots and the beneficial effect of the rootstock will be lost. Be careful not to injure the bark while planting, or bacterial canker may set in. Keep the soil round the tree free of grass

FORMATIVE TRAINING OF PYRAMID PLUM TREE

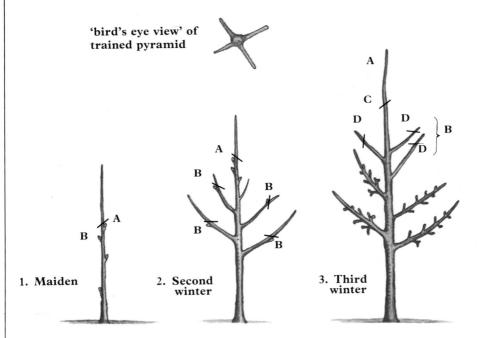

'bird's eye view' of trained pyramid

A
C
D   D
} B
D

1. Maiden

A
B
B
B
B
B

2. Second winter

3. Third winter

Pruning young pyramid trees should be done in the winter; because the wounds are tiny, the trees are unlikely to get silver leaf.

1. Cut the maiden back to 50 cm (20") the first winter the tree is in your garden. Cut back to a suitably placed bud (A). Rub out bud immediately below leader bud (B). Make sure there are 3 or 4 buds left spaced evenly around the stem.

2. The next winter, prune the leader to about 45 cm (18") to a bud pointing in the opposite direction from the previous year's pruning; this helps keep the growth straight (A). Make sure there are 3 well-placed buds on the remaining part of the leader to make a second whorl of branches. Prune all branches back to 22 cm (9") (B); this encourages the formation of fruit spurs.

3, 4. Train the leader vertically (A); the second whorl of branches will grow out (B). Cut back the sideshoots formed on the lower set of branches to 4 good leaves during early summer. In the third winter cut back the leader to 45 cm (18") (C) and the new whorl of branches back to 22 cm (9") (D).

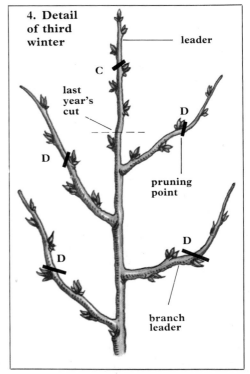

4. Detail of third winter

leader

C

last year's cut

D

D

pruning point

branch leader

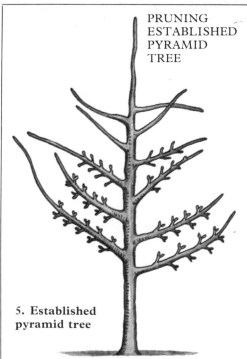

PRUNING ESTABLISHED PYRAMID TREE

5. Established pyramid tree

5, 6. *Plums need much less pruning than older fruit trees because they fruit on old and new wood. Generally, pruning should be done in early summer to avoid the risk of dieback and silver leaf. Pinch out vigorous sideshoots to 4 to 6 leaves from the parent stem (A and B). This encourages fruiting spurs to form. Cut out any dead wood back to living wood (C) and if the wound is larger than 2.5 cm (1″) treat it with bitumen paint. When the branch leaders grow longer than 1.2 m (4′), cut it back by one fourth to one third, depending on the vigour of the tree. Cut back to a suitably spaced spur or sideshoot (D). If the variety has a naturally drooping habit, such as* Victoria, *prune the branch leader back to an upward growing spur or sideshoot. Cutting back the branch leaders encourages the formation of new sideshoots. When the leader grows taller than 2.4 m (8′), cut it back into the old wood (E). Do this at blossom time, in mid-spring, every three or four years, as necessary.*

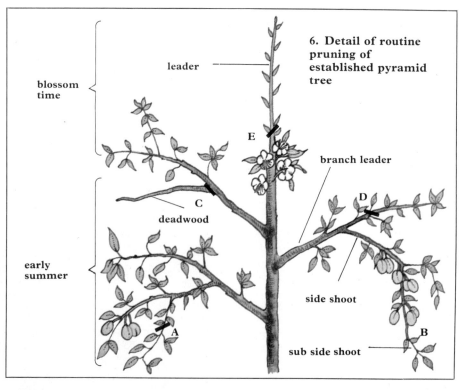

6. Detail of routine pruning of established pyramid tree

leader

blossom time

branch leader

C
deadwood

D

early summer

side shoot

A

B

sub side shoot

and weeds, so the plum does not have to compete with them for moisture during the summer.

If you are planting more than one tree, space less vigorous varieties, such as those on St. Julian A rootstock, 3 m (10') apart. Space pyramid trees and those on Myrobalan B rootstock 5.5 m (18') apart. Fan-trained trees on St. Julian A rootstock should be allowed at least 4.5 m (15') wall space.

Manuring and aftercare

Check frequently to make sure that newly planted trees have not been lifted by frost; firm down any which have been lifted. If the summer is dry, water any newly planted trees and also water established trees which are grown against a wall.

Plums need plenty of nitrogen, and should never run short of lime. A good mulch of rotted manure or compost, rich in nitrogen, is especially helpful to young trees, applied in mid-spring every year. Mulch an area of soil slightly larger than the area covered by the tree's branches.

In autumn, fork over the soil very lightly. Do not fork too deeply, because plums have very shallow rooting systems, closer to the surface than pears or apples, and over-vigorous forking may damage the roots.

The amount of fertilizer given varies according to the type of tree and soil conditions. A good general rule for trees growing normally in moderate to good soil is to apply 30 g per sq m (1 oz per sq yd) of nitro-chalk or sulphate of ammonia in late winter, and 15 g per sq m ($\frac{1}{2}$ oz per sq yd) of sulphate of potash in mid-autumn. About three years after planting, apply 30 g per sq m (1 oz per sq yd) superphosphate in late winter, and repeat at three-yearly intervals. Be careful not to overfertilize wall-trained trees, particularly with too much nitrogenous fertilizer, or lush unfruitful growth may result.

If you have no manure or compost available, mulch annually with moist peat to conserve soil moisture, and give twice as much nitro-chalk in the fertilizer mixture.

A major problem with plum trees is the continual production of root suckers, which use much of the nourishment needed by the tree. Check for suckers whenever pruning the tree. Carefully dig away the soil until you can see where the sucker joins the root, then pull the sucker off to remove the adventitious buds around it. Do not cut the sucker, as it is impossible not to leave a bud or two behind. Any injury to the root will heal quickly.

Pruning

One general rule applies to any pruning done to plum trees. Because of the risk of infection by silver leaf disease during the early autumn and late spring months, all pruning should either be carried out in winter on young trees, when the wounds are small and the trees vigorous, or immediately after fruiting in the summer or in the beginning of early autumn for older trees. Whenever you prune, make sure all large cuts (over 2.5 cm, or 1″ in diameter) are flush with the bark and covered with a protective sealer. Remove and burn dead or diseased wood, and shorten any unduly long shoots at this time.

Plums form fruit buds along the whole length of younger branches so, aside from cutting out dead wood and thinning overcrowded branches, pruning should be kept to a minimum. An established plum tree can carry a much larger proportion of wood than other fruit trees, and drastic pruning is never necessary.

Ready-trained bush, half-standard and standard trees are available at nurseries. Pyramid trained trees are smaller than standards and half-standards and can be grown in restricted areas. A pyramid-trained tree has an upright trunk with branches radiating out in all directions, like a Christmas tree. This form is relatively easy to pick and net against birds.

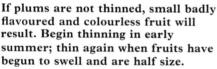

If plums are not thinned, small badly flavoured and colourless fruit will result. Begin thinning in early summer; thin again when fruits have begun to swell and are half size.

The final distance between fruit should be 5–7.5 cm (2–3″), or more for larger varieties, so the fully developed plums do not touch.

Thinning fruit

Plums tend to crop too heavily one year and too lightly the next. An excessively heavy crop usually means small, colourless and tasteless fruit. In varieties with very brittle wood, like *Victoria,* broken branches can result. To get fruit of the best size and flavour, thin the fruit in two stages. Begin thinning in early summer, then thin again after the tree has shed some of the fruit naturally at the stone-hardening stage. The fruits at the second thinning should be swelling and about half their final size. When thinning fruits, always remove diseased, injured or badly shaped plums first. Try to aim for 5–7.5 cm (2–3″) of space between the fruits. Allow 10 cm (4″) or more for varieties with very large fruit, so that

plums can develop fully without touching each other. Do not remove the stalk with the top fruit, as the shoot could be harmed and next year's crop may be damaged as a result.

Supporting branches

Any heavy-bearing branches must be supported, because even after thinning the weight of the crop can be considerable. One method of support is to drive in a heavy, upright stake next to the trunk, and support the branches by ropes attached to the top of the stake, like a maypole. You can also support individual branches from below by driving in stakes which are forked at the top. Wrap the branch with sacking where it meets the crotch to avoid

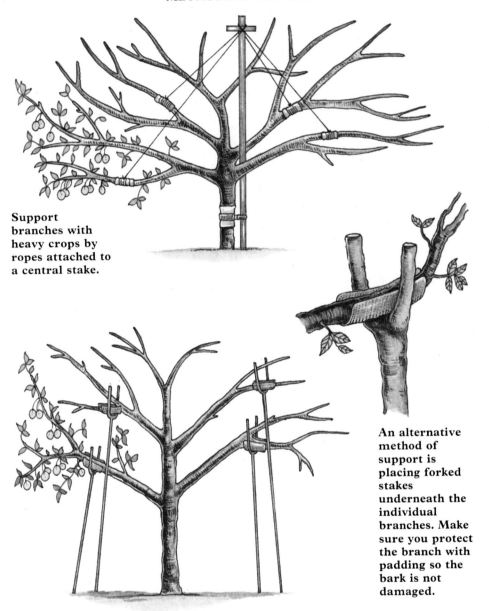

Support branches with heavy crops by ropes attached to a central stake.

An alternative method of support is placing forked stakes underneath the individual branches. Make sure you protect the branch with padding so the bark is not damaged.

chafing and subsequent risk of disease.

Growing plums in pots

Plums, particularly the late-fruiting dessert varieties, are suitable for growing in large pots or tubs. Make sure you select a tree with a semi-dwarfing rootstock. Pyramid, fan-trained or bush are the best sizes for pot culture.

Start the trees in pots in early autumn, preferably in 35 cm (14″) pots. Put crocks or broken bricks at the bottom, so the drainage hole is kept open. For the potting mixture, combine (by volume) five parts fibrous loam, one part decayed manure, one part lime or old mortar rubble, and one-half part peat or leafmould. Add 8 g ($\frac{1}{4}$ oz) sulphate of potash for each pot and mix thoroughly into the compost. When planting the tree, fill the pot to within 5 cm (2") of the rim. Find the sunniest and most sheltered site for the plant, against a wall if possible.

The cultivation for pot-grown plums is similar to that for open grown plums, with a few exceptions.

Make sure the soil in the pots never dries out; water daily in summer if necessary. Syringe the foliage with water from early summer onwards. Mulching the plants with moist peat will help retain moisture. In early autumn of each year, remove some of the old compost from the top few inches and replace it with fresh. In the winter, protect the roots from frost by covering the soil in the pots with leaf litter or dried bracken. Wrap some protective material, such as several sheets of newspaper or fibreglass with polythene, around the pots. From early summer to early autumn, feed weekly with dilute liquid manure. Lastly, you will get a heavier crop if you hand pollinate the blossom with a camelhair brush several times during the flowering season.

Harvesting

Trees begin bearing fruit when they are about five years old, and cropping is from late mid-summer to late autumn, depending on the variety. Leave dessert fruit on the tree until it is thoroughly ripe to obtain the best flavour. For jam-making, bottling, and ordinary cooking, it is best to pick the fruit while it is slightly under-ripe.

Both dessert and cooking varieties should be picked several times as they ripen; do not clear the tree at one picking. Most varieties can be easily detached from the stalk when ripe, but some types, particularly gages and damsons, are easier to pick with the stalks still attached. Take care not to jerk them off, as this can damage the shoots. Always remove and destroy any dam-

aged and rotting fruit you come across while harvesting. Do not allow them to remain on the tree, or brown rot may result.

Gages and some other varieties are liable to split in wet weather. If heavy rain threatens and the fruit is nearly ripe, pick the fruit and bring it indoors to ripen. This may impair the flavour a little, but you will avoid cracked fruits, which are often inedible.

Storing

Ripe plums picked in the ordinary way will not keep for more than a couple of days. If you want to keep plums for a longer period, pick them when they are dry, slightly under-ripe and with the stalks still attached. Use secateurs to cut the stalk from the spur, to avoid the risk of tearing the bark. Wrap the fruit carefully, and place it in one layer in a shallow basket or box, making sure that the plums are not touching each other. Put the box or basket in a cool airy place; the fruit should keep for two to three weeks.

Exhibition tips

For both cooking and dessert plums, the judges will look for large, fully ripe fruits with the stalks intact. They should have a good colour and undamaged bloom. Small, under-ripe or over-ripe fruits or those lacking stalks will be considered defective.

After picking the plums you wish to exhibit, wrap them individually in tissues and store them in a cool place until the show. Make sure your pre-sentation of plums is neat and attractive. Do not, however, polish the plums or the bloom will be lost. Lay the plums in lines across the plate, with the stalks pointing away from the front of the table. Nine is the usual number of plums shown; they all should be of the same variety unless otherwise stated in the schedule. Damsons and bullaces are a separate category of exhibit, but the same criteria apply. Usually, however, thirty damsons or bullaces are shown, instead of nine.

Varieties

As explained above, a number of varieties need to be cross-pollinated by another variety with a coincidental flowering period. Where necessary, we have indicated suitable pollinators.

Gages

Early Transparent: dessert; medium round, apricot yellow fruit; excellent flavour; fruits late summer; *self-fertile.*

Denniston's Superb: dessert; pale green with red flush; delicious flavour; reliable

Victoria

cropper in late summer; *self-fertile.*

Oullin's Golden Gage: dessert; fruits golden yellow; crops late summer; *self-fertile.*

Cambridge: dessert; fruits similar to old-fashioned greengage, but better cropper; crops in late summer; self-fertile but cropping improved by cross-pollination with *Victoria, Czar, Golden Transparent,* or *Laxton's Gage.*

Jefferson's Gage: dessert; yellow-green with bronze markings; juicy and delicious fruit; crops early autumn; *cross-pollinate* with *Denniston's Superb* or *Early Transparent.*

Damsons

Merryweather Damson: cooking; big, well flavoured fruit; good for bottling or freezing; crops early autumn; *self-fertile.*

Quetsche: cooking; medium-sized purple fruit; crops mid-autumn; *self-fertile.*

Plums

Early Laxton: cooking and dessert; very prolific; earliest plum; small, yellowish red fruits, better for cooking than eating; crops mid-summer; *cross-pollinate* with *Czar, Victoria* or *Merryweather Damson.*

River's Early Prolific: cooking; small, roundish purple fruit; reliable cropper in mid-summer, *cross-pollinate* with *Czar, Victoria,* or *Merryweather Damson.*

Czar: cooking; reddish purple fruit; hardy, prolific and frost-resistant; *self-fertile.*

Yellow Pershore: cooking; medium-sized, golden-yellow fruit; crops in late summer; *self-fertile.*

Victoria: cooking and dessert; heavy cropper, excellent flavour; crops early autumn; *self-fertile.*

Warwickshire Drooper: cooking; medium to large yellow egg-shaped fruit; crops mid-summer; *self-fertile.*

Coe's Golden Drop: dessert; golden yellow, spotted red; crops mid-autumn; *cross-pollinate* with *Early Transparent Gage, Early Laxton* or *Denniston's Early.*

Marjorie's Seedling: dessert and cooking; large, oval purple fruit, flesh pale yellow; vigorous grower, good cropper; crops mid-autumn; *self-fertile.*

Ariel: dessert; oval, yellow-green fruit with pink flush; reliable cropper; crops early autumn; *self-fertile.*

Kirke's Blue: dessert; rich flavoured, large, round blue fruit; light cropper; does best in sheltered position; *cross-pollinate* with *Czar* or *Victoria.*

Belle de Louvain: cooking; large, oval rich-flavoured fruit; crops late summer, *self-fertile.*

Giant Prune: dessert; large red fruit crops early autumn; *self-fertile.*

Pests & Diseases

Birds: can do the most damage to both buds and fruit. Net small trees and place glitterbangs or other scaring devices on large trees.

Leaf-curling plum aphids: these are particularly prolific pests, often producing three generations in one season. In spring the aphids completely cover the undersides of leaves, which curl and die. The aphids also excrete honeydew, which leads to infection by sooty mould. Control with tar oil washes in winter. If the aphids appear in spring, spray the trees with derris or malathion before the leaves have curled.

Plum sawfly: caterpillars of the plum sawfly eat their way into the young fruits, and a sticky black substance exudes from the holes they have made. If the infection is severe, cropping will be considerably reduced. Spray with fenitrothion or derris one week after petal-fall.

Red plum maggot: this relative of the codling moth eats its way into the fruit, like the plum sawfly, but it appears much later in the season. Eggs are laid at the base of the fruit stalk, and the emerging red caterpillars attack the young fruits. The best way to control red plum maggot is to kill caterpillars in cocoons in mid-winter by spraying the trees with a tar oil wash. If the moths are seen in early to mid-summer, spray with derris about a week after their first appearance.

Plum gall mites: these microscopic creatures overwinter in the bud scales and emerge in spring to attack the leaves. They produce pouch-shaped blisters in the leaves, which may eventually curl up and die. Spray in late winter with $\frac{1}{2}$ L lime sulphur to $13\frac{1}{2}$ L water (1 pt lime sulphur to $3\frac{3}{4}$ gal water). Check the trees frequently in summer for leaves which have blisters on them. Pick off and burn

Plum leaf sawfly: this pest occasionally attacks plums, feeding on the leaves from early summer to early autumn. The larvae are slug-like, yellowish-white later changing to dark green or black, and they usually attack the upper surfaces of the leaves, which become blotchy and skeletonized. Apply derris or fenitrothion washes or dusts in early summer if you see large numbers of larvae.

Red spider mite: these tiny mites infest the undersides of the leaves and feed on the sap. Infected leaves will turn brown and fall prematurely. Red spider overwinters on the tree as eggs laid in the crevices of bark; a late winter wash of DNOC/petroleum will usually kill the eggs. If red spider mite does appear, from late spring onwards, spray with malathion, dimethoate or derris.

Silver leaf: this disease is caused by a fungus and is a major problem with plum trees. *Victoria* is particularly susceptible. The disease is called 'silver leaf' because leaves of infected trees develop a silvery sheen. A second symptom of the disease is a purple-brown stain in the wood when cut across. A final symptom of the disease is the appearance of brown or purple fungal fruiting bodies on the wood. Once this fungus appears, the tree should be removed and destroyed, as it will never recover. As soon as a tree develops silver leaf, cut back the infected wood until no purple-brown staining can be seen. Then apply lime and fertilizer to keep the tree vigorous, as healthier trees have a better chance of

Iron deficiency: although plums need only a small amount of iron, if it is lacking the trees cannot manufacture chlorophyll and will suffer from chlorosis. This occurs most frequently on very chalky soils. The main symptom is a yellowing of the leaves well before autumn. Correct this by dressing the soil with 120 g per sq m (4 oz per sq yd) of iron sulphate. Try to avoid planting on chalky soils.

Bacterial canker: this is a serious infection, and appears first in early summer as brown spots on the leaves. These spots develop into holes, and this stage of infection is sometimes called 'shothole'. Cankers later develop on the branches or trunk of the tree; these long, cracking areas ooze gum. If the canker encircles the entire stem, the tree will die. The following spring, buds on infected branches may not open; if leaves do appear, they are small and yellow and soon die. There is no chemical way to control bacterial canker. Avoid pruning the tree during autumn and winter, when the infection is most likely to occur. Protect any pruning wounds with a coat of sealer. Always avoid damage to the trunk of the branches by making sure stakes are not rubbing the bark. *Victoria* is one of the varieties most susceptible.

Honey fungus: this very damaging disease attacks the roots of trees and can quickly kill them. Trees on heavy, badly drained soils are most likely to be affected, so make sure you have corrected any drainage problems before planting. Another good preventive measure is to make sure you have removed all nearby dead tree stumps and hedgerows before planting, as the fungus lives in dead and dying wood. Lastly, make sure the stakes anchoring the tree have been dipped in creosote or other wood preservative.

As the fungus attacks the plant via the roots, there are few noticeable signs above ground, however premature autumn colouring and leaf fall may be symptoms. Trees which are seemingly healthy and then die for no apparent reason should be dug up and inspected. Lift the bark just below ground level. If you see among the roots and in the soil long, shiny black strands, then honey fungus is present. It is these black strands which reach out, underground, to infect nearby plants.

Dig up and burn infected trees, including all the root system. Use a different site when replacing tree.

Brown rot: this disease attacks other top fruits besides plums. It appears as small brown patches, inside which are circular rings, whitish or yellow in colour. These rings contain the spores, which spread the disease to other fruit, particularly if the fruit are damaged by birds or insects. Infected plums may drop off the tree, or else remain on the tree shrivelled up. If they remain mummified on the tree all winter, they will reinfect the next season's fruit. Remove and burn any diseased fruit, both on the tree and on the ground. As the infection can spread down the stalk to the fruiting spur, cut off the infected spur when removing mummified fruit.

Pocket plum: this is also known as bladder plum, or plum pocket. It is a fungal disease which causes the young fruit to grow long, swollen and one-sided. The skin of the fruit eventually develops a whitish bloom. Cut off all infected fruit and the attached shoots, as the infection spreads to the wood.

GUIDE TO PLUM TROUBLES

Symptoms	*Probable causes*
Leaves curl and die	Leaf-curling plum aphids
Holes in fruit oozing sticky black substance	Plum sawfly
Holes eaten in fruit in mid-summer	Red plum maggot
Pouch-shaped blisters on leaves	Plum gall mite
Blotchy, skeletonized leaves	Pear slug sawfly
Bronzed leaves, premature leaf-fall	Red spider mite
Leaves silvery, wood stained brown	Silver leaf
Leaves yellow prematurely	Iron deficiency
Spots on leaves, cracking bark	Bacterial canker
Fruits long, swollen and one-sided	Pocket plum
Trees die, black strands in soil and among roots	Honey fungus
Brown patches on fruit which shrivels up on tree	Brown rot

Raspberries

Rubus idaeus (fam. *Rosaceae*)
Hardy perennial prickly cane with a
useful life of 12 years
Size: up to 2.5 m (8′) high unpruned;
kept to about 1.2-1.5 m (4-5′) when fruiting
Yield: 1.5-3 kg (3-7 lb) per stool or
11-22 kg (25-49 lb) per 3 m (10′) row
Planting to harvesting time: 2 years

Of all soft fruit, raspberries are most
suited to home growing. As they do not
travel or keep well, raspberries freshly
picked from your garden are likely to be
far superior in quality and taste to store-
bought ones. This is because most
commercial varieties are not particularly
flavourful, but have been bred to
produce fruit which have the ability to
withstand the rigours of packing and
transport. The old variety *Lloyd George,*
which is universally considered to be the
best tasting raspberry, is rarely available
in the shops because the berries quickly
lose their shape once picked. By growing
your own, you can choose from a wide
range of flavourful varieties, and by
planting for successional cropping, you
can enjoy fresh raspberries from early
summer through to the first autumn
frosts.

Raspberries give very quick returns,
and are second only to strawberries in
the length of time from planting until
cropping. Although they will produce
some fruit the first season they are
planted, it is best not to allow them to do
so. By pinching out the flowers as they
appear, you are encouraging the young

plants to develop strong stools and root
systems instead of fruiting, and the canes
should then produce heavy crops from
the second season onwards. Unlike
strawberries, which are disease-prone
and need replanting every three years or
so, well cultivated raspberry canes will
continue to be fruitful for at least twelve
years.

The plant itself, *Rubus idaeus*, is a
native of Europe, including Britain, and
parts of Asia. It can often be found
growing wild in hedgerows and on hilly
heathland with acid soils. Many of these
plants are garden escapes, the seeds
having been scattered by birds. Although most raspberries have red or
purplish-red berries, there are richly-
flavoured yellow-fruited varieties (sometimes known as white raspberries) and
also black raspberries. These black-
fruited types, derived from *R. occiden-
talis,* are much more popular in America
than Europe, and are widely cultivated
there. Unlike the raspberry, which has a
spreading habit of growth, black raspberries are clump-forming, with heavier
and more branched canes.

Raspberries flower and fruit on

1. In mid-autumn, plant canes about 7.5 cm (3″) deep; spread roots out and firm soil thoroughly.

2. After planting, cut canes back to a strong healthy bud, about 30 cm (1′) above ground.

laterals growing from canes which were produced the previous year, after which the fruiting canes die, and are replaced by new canes. Although most varieties fruit in mid-summer, there are some types which are specifically cultivated for autumn crops. These autumn fruiting, or everbearing, raspberries produce fruit on the tips of the current season's shoots. Fruit quantity may be smaller than that of summer fruiting canes. Summer and autumn fruiting varieties require slightly different methods of pruning, but neither method is particularly difficult or time consuming. The variety *Lloyd George* can be pruned to crop early, mid-season or in autumn, and traditionally some bushes in the fruit cage were pruned for early cropping and the rest pruned for maincrop and late picking.

Suitable site and soil

Raspberries do best in a sunny site, but being woodland plants, they will tolerate some shade. Because they flower relatively late in the season, frost is not usually damaging and low-lying sites can be satisfactory for growing raspberries in most years, unless there is a very late frost. They will not tolerate waterlogged soil, however, and in very wet winters, excessive water will kill the roots.

Besides soil drainage, shelter from wind is the second major consideration. The canes are fairly brittle and may snap off in high winds, and the point where the fruiting laterals join the canes is also very vulnerable to serious damage from strong winds.

The best soils are deep, rich, well-drained loams, as long as they retain some moisture in dry weather. Shallow sands and gravels can be made suitable, if you are prepared to water them frequently and give a continual supply of nutrients. Likewise, heavy clay soils are not really suitable without careful preparation and maintenance, because they tend to harden and crack in dry summers depriving the shallow roots of water. Raspberries will accept more acid conditions than most other soft fruits, but readily become chlorotic in too alkaline a soil. Shallow soils over chalk should be avoided.

Because some viral infections are soil-borne by eelworms, avoid planting new canes in sites previously occupied by berries of the same genus and plant as far away as possible from old fruiting canes.

Begin soil preparation well in advance. Remember that the plants will remain in the ground for at least 12 years and no amount of aftercare will make up for inadequate preparation. Whatever the soil type, make sure the ground is completely free from perennial weeds, such as couch, bindweed and nettles. If the subsoil is hard and impervious to water, break it up with a fork. Then fork in well-rotted manure at the rate of 12 L (2½ gal) per plant. At the same time, apply superphosphate, at the rate of 30 g per sq m (1 oz per sq yd). If manure is not available, use garden compost, leaf-mould or moist peat. If the soil is very alkaline, and using it for raspberries is unavoidable, work in fritted trace elements at the time of planting at the rates recommended by the suppliers, and thereafter treat the plants as suggested under PESTS AND DISEASES.

Planting out

Buy canes which are certified virus-free and plant in mid-autumn. Because raspberries break into fresh growth very early in spring, later plantings should be avoided. If, however, the ground is very wet or cold when the canes arrive, you can heel them in until conditions are more suitable.

Dig out a shallow trench about 30 cm (1′) wide where the row is to be. Space the canes 45 cm (18″) apart; if you have more than one row, leave a minimum of 1.5 m (5′) between rows. This may seem wasteful of space, but the canes must be exposed to enough air and sunlight for the fruits to ripen properly. Closer planting will also encourage problems with pests and diseases. If you are planting varieties which are slow to sucker, such as *Lloyd George,* you can plant two canes per station.

Plant the canes firmly, with the roots well spread out and about 7.5 cm (3″) deep; there should be a soil mark on the stems indicating the right planting depth. After planting, either at once or some time before spring, cut the canes back to a strong healthy bud about 30 cm (1′) above ground. This may seem a bit drastic, but if you do not cut the cane back, and allow it to fruit in the first season, the plant's ability to produce vigorous new canes will be seriously

reduced, and it will not crop properly for another two years.

Should there be any heavy frosts after planting, check the newly planted canes; if any have been lifted by frost, firm them down.

Erecting training wires

There are two basic methods of support. The quicker method, as it does not involve tying individual canes, is to have two rows of parallel wires through which the canes grow. To do this, erect stout end posts, at a maximum distance of 5 m (16′) apart. At 60 cm (2′) and again at 1.5 m (5′) bolt on to the end posts cross pieces of wood about 30 cm (1′) long, to act as spacers. Then run wires (telephone wire is best) from one cross piece to the other, fixed with a strainer at each end (see diagram). The young canes are then trained to grow up between the wires, and the canes inside the wires tend to support each other. There is one disadvantage to this system: in high winds, serious damage can occur, and if the canes get too overcrowded, they are more vulnerable to disease.

The slightly more time-consuming, but better method of support is to tie the canes individually to parallel horizontal wires as they grow. Drive 2.25 m (7½′) poles 45 cm (1½′) into the ground at each end of the row. The first autumn after planting, erect horizontal wires at 45 cm (1½′), 105 cm (3½′) and 1.2-1.5 m (4-5′) depending on the vigour of the variety. Then tie the young canes individually to the bottom wire with soft garden twine, and to the middle and upper wires as soon as they are tall enough.

Training and pruning

The young canes grow from adventitious buds; without training or pruning the plant would quickly form an impenetrable thicket of stems. Because the root system is very wide-spreading, new canes may appear some distance from the parent plant.

The first summer after planting, cut out the old canes entirely when the

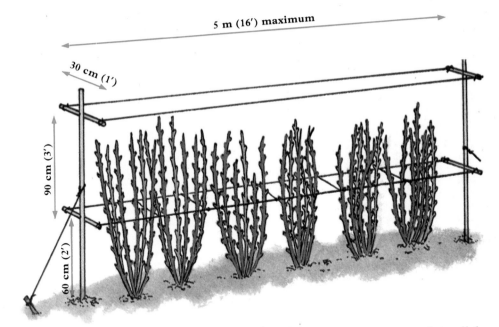

5 m (16') maximum

30 cm (1')

90 cm (3')

60 cm (2')

To support raspberries without tying individual canes, erect two rows of parallel wires through which canes grow; fix wires to cross-pieces at end posts.

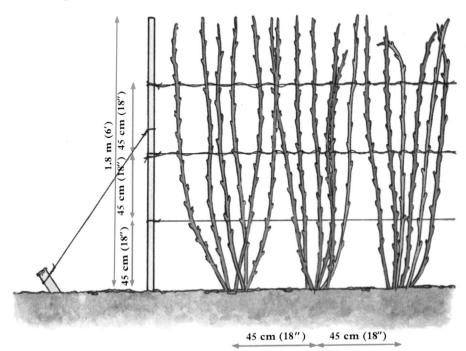

1.8 m (6')

45 cm (18")

45 cm (18")

45 cm (18")

45 cm (18")   45 cm (18")

Alternatively, tie canes individually to parallel horizontal wires as they grow. Erect wires at 45 cm (18"), 90 cm (3') and 1.2-1.5 m (4-5') from ground.

1. In the first summer after planting, when the young canes are 25 cm (10″) high, cut out old canes entirely.

2. As the canes grow, tie them to bottom wire with soft twine, and then to middle and upper wires.

young canes reach 25 cm (10″) high. The following late winter, tip prune all the canes slightly. Strong growing ones should be cut back to a good bud about 15 cm (6″) above the top wire; less strong growing canes should have the top 7.5-10 cm (3-4″) removed. This winter tipping, which should be done annually, will get rid of any diseased and damaged cane tips, and it will also encourage the canes to send out more fruiting laterals, thus increasing crop yields.

Healthy raspberry stools will normally produce more canes than are practical for good cultivation, so from the second summer onwards, allow only six fruiting canes per stool, choosing the strongest. If you remove all the weak, damaged or diseased canes early in the season, the selected fruiting canes will have more room to grow and more sunlight. Tie these six to the wires to keep them separated and firm. While these are flowering and fruiting, new shoots will appear and, as before, the obvious weak ones are cut out, and the best of the remainder left as replacements, to bear the following year's fruit.

After cropping, cut to the ground the old fruiting canes; it is a good idea to remove and burn them immediately, to lessen the possibility of disease. Then tie in the selected young canes which have

grown during the spring and summer for next year.

Autumn-fruiting varieties are pruned by cutting the old canes down to ground level in late winter or early spring; the plant will then produce canes in spring and summer on which fruit will be produced in autumn.

Care and cultivation

If dry weather occurs when the plants are flowering, watering is essential. Otherwise the new canes, which are growing at the same time, will be small and sparse, and next year's crop will be poor. An annual mulch of well-rotted compost or manure in mid-spring will help conserve soil moisture. If the soil is dry, water it thoroughly before mulching. Because the roots are shallow and wide-spreading, the mulch should be spread 1 m (1 yd) on either side of the row. A good rule of thumb is to apply 2.5 kg (5 lb) of mulch per sq m (sq yd).

Weeds, which compete with the canes for moisture and nutrients, must be controlled. Over-vigorous hoeing can do more harm than good, though, because the shallow roots are very near the surface. Hand weeding is better. Remove unwanted suckers which may spring up between the rows, unless you want them for propagation, and cut back

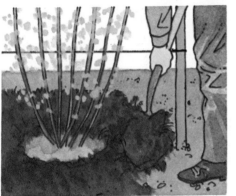

3. Mulch in mid-spring with garden compost or well-rotted manure to keep weeds down and conserve soil moisture.

4. If bushes are not growing in a fruit cage, give temporary protection when fruit begins to form. Use 2.5 cm (1″) nylon mesh netting over stout wooden posts. Bricks will keep net from blowing away in strong wind.

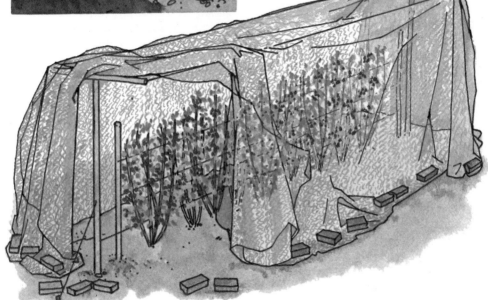

5. Harvest on dry sunny days. Support laterals with one hand while picking berries with the other.

6. Put berries in shallow bowls or punnets, so they are not crushed by their own weight.

1. Tip prune in winter: cut strong-growing canes back to a good bud 15 cm (6″) above top wire.

2. After fruiting, cut old canes back to ground level in autumn; remove and burn canes immediately.

to the ground all small or spindly canes.

Under good conditions, raspberries will not require extra fertilizer, but if cane production is inadequate, fertilizer should be applied in late winter. Scatter a nitrogenous one, such as sulphate of ammonia, at the rate of 30-45 g per sq m (1-1½ oz per sq yd), and one containing potassium, eg sulphate of potash, at 15-30 g per sq m (½-1 oz per sq yd).

The raspberry is a favourite target for birds, and netting is the only satisfactory long-term solution.

Growing black raspberries

Newly planted canes of black raspberry varieties are best cut off at ground level after planting. Young canes produced during the first growing year are cut back during the summer to 50-75 cm (20-30″) high to stimulate the growth of side-shoots. The following late winter or early spring these are also cut back to leave two to six buds, depending on the strength of the cane; the stronger shoots can support more buds. Fruiting branches are produced from these buds. It is not necessary to provide support for black raspberries, but they can be tied in for convenience. In the second and subsequent years, the primary canes should be limited to four per stool, preferably by early selection or during

the post-harvest clean up. Tipping off the main shoots and cutting back of the sideshoots continues each year.

Propagation

Raspberries can be easily propagated from suckers which spring up at or near the base of the parent plant. This is a somewhat risky business, though, because if the parent plants are not absolutely healthy, the newly propagated canes will be diseased from the start. To avoid all risk, you should not propagate new canes from your own fruiting stock, but buy in fresh certified virus-free stock from a reputable source.

If you do want to propagate new canes from your own stock, autumn is the best time to do so. Gently loosen the rooted suckers which have grown during the season with a fork and sever them from the parent plant. The suckers should have strong, well-developed root systems: discard those without much root and those which have weak or spindly growth. Plant the suckers out in their permanent positions and immediately cut them back to 60 cm (2′) above ground. The following late winter or early spring, cut the canes back again, to a strong bud about 30 cm (1′) above ground. The American black raspberry is propagated by tip layering. Wait until

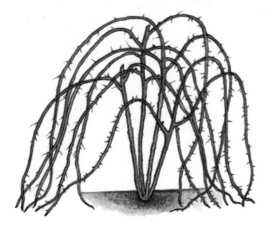

Black raspberry before spring pruning; the main canes have been stopped during the first year of growth.

To prune, cut the laterals back to two to six buds, depending on the strength of each cane.

the side branches are long enough to touch the ground without snapping; this is usually in early to mid-summer. Dig out a 15 cm (6″) deep hole for each branch you are tip layering; the holes should have side slopes of about 45°. If the soil is very heavy, it is best to put a little bit of moist peat mixed with sand into the bottom of the hole; this will encourage root formation. Then gently place the tip of the branch into the hole, against the sloping side, so that about 15 cm (6″) of cane is buried. Backfill with soil and tread down firmly. Peg the cane

The easiest way to propagate new plants is from suckers: sever them with a sharp spade, in late autumn.

where it enters the soil with a metal or wooden peg, to keep it from springing up.

The following autumn, after cropping is finished, sever the rooted cane from the parent plant with a sharp spade, and transplant it to its permanent position.

Harvesting
The early fruiting varieties should be ready for harvesting early in mid-summer, and should continue for three weeks. The maincrop varieties follow, then come the autumn-fruiting types. Pick the berries in dry weather. The fruit does not ripen all at once, so inspect canes every other day. Normally, the fruit is picked without the central core.

Raspberries do not keep for very long, so eat them or preserve them without delay.

Exhibition tips
Thirty is the usual number of fruit required, all of the same variety. Always pick the raspberries with the stalk intact. In taking them to the show, pack in a single layer in a box, and cover with tissue paper. Arrange neatly on a plate to exhibit. The judges will look for large ripe fruit in good condition.

Varieties

Early

Malling Promise: first raspberry to fruit in early summer; good flavour and strong growth (to 2.1 m (7′)), but takes a couple of years to settle down; frost-resistant but fruit susceptible to botrytis; large, good for jam.

Malling Exploit: more vigorous than *Malling Promise* and probably more widely planted; fruit very large but tends to be crumbly, very fine flavoured; thrives in a wide range of soils.

Glen Cova: medium-sized berry; excellent for bottling or freezing; crops start early and continue over several weeks with heavy mid-season yield.

Malling Jewel: second early; medium-sized, dark red fruit, somewhat hidden by leaves curling over it; 'flavour excellent; somewhat frost and botrytis resistant; most popular raspberry for general use; growth compact and less liable to wind damage.

Mid-season

Lloyd George (New Zealand Strain): original *Lloyd George* strain decimated by virus, but replaced by clean stocks from New Zealand; best flavoured raspberry, but difficult to grow well; crops early, mid-season, and again on tips of young canes in autumn; very prone to viral infection and may need replacing after a few years.

Malling Orion: recent introduction; fruit medium large and round; flavour good; consistently heavy cropper over long period of time.

Phyllis King: old variety recently re-introduced; berries large, firm and well flavoured.

Malling 'M': mid- to late variety with fruit excellent for bottling.

Malling Delight: recently introduced heavy cropper with large long berries; not suitable for freezing.

Golden Everest: yellow-fruited variety with mild, delicious flavour; fruits over a long season on both old and young canes.

Malling Promise

Late

Norfolk Giant: crops a week later than maincrop; fruit of good flavour and texture, but a bit acid for dessert; tall-growing variety, susceptible to wind damage, frost damage and virus; particularly good for jam-making and bottling or freezing.

Malling Admiral: recent introduction; heavier cropper than *Norfolk Giant.*

Autumn

September: American variety with very firm, well-flavoured fruit; for autumn cropping, canes must be cut to ground level in winter or early spring; growth thick and vigorous but unsuitable for colder northern districts; will crop well on dry soils and in dry seasons.

Zeva: Swiss variety with unusually large fruit; yields well in first year of cropping; crops from mid-summer until late autumn, with heaviest crop in autumn.

Sceptre: vigorous variety, giving high autumn yields under most conditions.

Heritage: most vigorous of autumn-fruiting varieties; sturdy, self-supporting canes, fruit first class with good flavour.

Black raspberries

Blackie: cross between thorny blackberry and raspberry; limited supplies.

Pests & Diseases

Raspberry beetle: raspberry beetle is probably the most serious pest you are likely to encounter, and bad attacks may render your crop inedible. The female beetle, which is light brown and 0.4 cm ($\frac{1}{6}''$) long, lays her eggs in the open flower, in late spring and early summer, and the emerging maggots feed on the developing fruit. One of the worst aspects of this infestation is that it is not likely to be noticed until the raspberries are actually on the table. To control, spray with derris about fourteen days after flowering, at the fruitlet stage.

Aphids: · there are several species of aphid which infest raspberries, but the most serious are the raspberry aphid and the rubus aphid, both of which transmit viral diseases. They are present in their largest numbers in late spring and early summer, and their feeding results in the leaves curling a little, but they do not themselves do any great damage. It is their ability to spread virus diseases which is the really troublesome aspect of their infestations. If you have had serious trouble with aphids in previous years, apply a mid-winter spray of tar oil mixture to kill any overwintering eggs. Otherwise, if aphids appear, spray with malathion or dimethoate in spring before the flowers open, and again if necessary, but not while the plants are flowering. Remember to allow the specified time to lapse between spraying and harvesting.

Birds: unfortunately, birds find ripening raspberries particularly tempting, and although bird scarers provide some measure of relief, the only really effective long term protection is growing the crop in fruit cages.

Cane midge: this pest affects primarily young canes, which will have brownish-black blotches if infested. The grubs of the cane midge emerge in about early summer from eggs laid in cracks at the base of the canes and then begin to feed on the internal tissue of the cane. There may be two more broods in the season. Besides causing some physical

Ministry of Agriculture, Fisheries & Food

Cane spot: a fungal infection which damages canes, and causes spotted, mis-shapen fruit.

damage, the scars from the cane midge larva make the plants more vulnerable to secondary fungal infections. Some varieties seem more at risk than others; *Malling Enterprise* is very susceptible. To control cane midge, spray the young canes with gamma-HCH during late spring, and again two weeks later.

Raspberry moth: if the tips of young lateral shoots appear withered and tunnelled in late spring, then it is likely your canes are infested with caterpillars of the raspberry moth. The best preventive measure is keeping the raspberry bed clean and weed free, and removing withered shoots as soon as seen, because the grub, or chrysalis, is likely to be inside it. In severe cases, a winter tar oil wash applied to the soil at the foot of the canes should kill the hibernating larvae.

Capsids: these pests vary from year to year in numbers and the amount of damage done. The tips of young canes are most vulnerable to capsid attack; infested tips may stop growing altogether or form branches. Leaves are injured, and develop puckered brown spots and tiny holes, eventually becoming very tattered. As with aphids, a spray of dimethoate or malathion before the flowers open (treating the ground round the plants as well) is usually the most effective method of control.

Spur blight attacks buds on young canes; the infection spreads back to the stem.

Grey mould *(Botrytis cinerea)*: this is more likely to be troublesome with strawberries than raspberries, but the latter can be infected, particularly if they are growing in wet, overcrowded conditions. Berries with botrytis will be covered with grey, fluffy mould, and the canes can also be infected and even killed outright in severe cases. The best preventive measure is to plant the canes at the correct spacing, so that air can circulate freely. Cut off and burn all infected fruit and canes as soon as you notice them. In severe cases, spray with captan or benomyl when the first flowers open and again a fortnight later, but do not spray if the fruit is to be used for preserving in any way.

Cane blight: this fungal infection appears on the fruiting canes in summer; *Norfolk Giant* and *Lloyd George* are particularly susceptible. The main symptoms are wilted and withered leaves, and very brittle canes with dark basal patches which easily snap off at ground level. Small, dark, round fruiting bodies may appear on the bases of infected canes. Because raspberries attacked by cane midge larvae are very susceptible, the best precaution is to keep the garden clean, and so free of cane midges. All infected canes should be cut out, below ground level if possible, and burnt. This is particularly important in the case of canes which have snapped off, as the stump remaining in the ground can spread the infection. In the following spring spray the remaining canes with Bordeaux mixture or benomyl at bud burst, and repeat just before flowering to protect the young canes. Make sure the new growth is well spaced out and not crowded. Because cane blight is also soil borne, never use canes from infected beds. Buying certified stock will insure that new canes are free from cane blight.

Cane spot: this fungal infection, although not as serious as cane blight, can still reduce raspberry crops. The main symptoms are small, round, purple spots on the canes in late spring or early summer; occasionally the fruits are spotted or mis-shapen. Infected leaves will have pale spots surrounded with a dark border. In time, the spots on the canes grow larger, become elongated and change to pale grey in the centre. Eventually the holes become sunken and cankered, with cracking in the centre. Cut out and burn badly infected canes, and spray the remainder with Bordeaux mixture. If you have had serious trouble with cane spot in the past, spray with a 5% lime-sulphur mixture or benomyl at bud burst, and repeat just before blossoming.

Spur blight: this can be quite serious, as the buds from which the fruiting laterals grow can be killed. Buds on young canes become infected first, and the infection spreads back to the stem. The infected cane nearest the bud turns purple and this patch is the first visual indication that infection has occurred. Later this changes to a greyish white. Fungal fruiting bodies appear in the centre of these grey areas as tiny black dots. By the following spring, the infected buds will either have been killed, or will soon wither and die after opening. As with cane spot and cane blight, cut out and burn infected canes, thin the remainder out and spray with Bordeaux mixture or benomyl.

Chlorosis: this physiological disorder is most often seen on plants which are growing in alkaline soils. Leaf tissue of affected plants will turn yellow, on the youngest leaves first if the trouble is due to a deficiency of iron, and later the older ones; eventually they turn almost white. Lack of manganese shows as a fairly regular, small yellow mottling on the older leaves. Lack of magnesium appears as purple brown patches on the older leaves. The best preventive measure is to correct alkalinity problems before planting. Plants which develop chlorosis can be treated with sequestrenes, applied according to manufacturer's instructions, or fritted trace elements can be applied. Manganese and magnesium sulphate can be applied as foliar sprays.

GUIDE TO RASPBERRY TROUBLES

Symptoms	Probable cause
Fruit tunnelled and eaten; white maggots present.	Raspberry beetle
Young shoots stunted, leaves curled.	Aphids
Ripening fruit torn and holed.	Birds
Brownish-black blotches on base of canes.	Raspberry cane midge
Tips of young shoots withered and tunnelled.	Raspberry moth
Tips of young canes stop growing or form branches.	Capsids
Fruit and canes covered with fluffy grey mould.	Grey mould
Canes brittle, snap off at ground level; leaves wilted and withered.	Cane blight
Small, round purple spots on canes; fruit spotted or mis-shapen.	Cane spot
Canes purple in patches round spurs, later become pale and covered with black fruiting bodies	Spur blight
Leaves yellow between veins; fall prematurely.	Chlorosis
Leaves striped yellow; wither and die; canes with long blue stripe.	Blue stripe wilt
Leaves mottled or spotted yellow; leaves and canes dwarfed or stunted; diminished fruit production.	Virus infections

Blue stripe wilt: this fungal infection lives in the roots and prevents sap from flowing through the plant normally. In early to mid-summer, leaves of infected plants become striped yellow. Eventually the yellow stripes turn brown, and the leaves wither and die; in severe cases the canes become marked with a bluish stripe longitudinally and eventually die back as well. The only option with blue stripe wilt is to dig up and destroy infected plants, so the disease does not spread.

Viruses: there are several types of viral infections to which raspberries are susceptible; this is further complicated by the fact that the same virus may have different symptoms on different cultivars. All virus infections are very serious, and the infected plants must be dug up and burnt as soon as the diagnosis is made. The most common virus is mosaic, which initially appears as yellow and pale green mottling or spots on the leaves. Eventually, the leaves become smaller, crumpled and distorted, the canes become stunted and cropping diminishes considerably. The plant does not necessarily die at once, but it will never recover completely or crop well again. Some varieties are much more vulnerable than others; *Lloyd George* is very susceptible. Less common is raspberry yellow dwarf virus; the main symptoms are stunted canes and linear yellow patterns on the leaves. Lastly, stunt and dwarf virus may cause trouble; infected plants may be only 60 cm (2′) tall and cropping nearly non-existant. This virus is spread by leaf hoppers, unlike most other viruses, which are carried by aphids.

With all viruses, the best preventive measure is to control the carriers of the disease: aphids and, very rarely, leaf hoppers. Where soil-living eelworms are the culprits, new stock should not be planted in ground so infested. If you can keep your garden free from these pests, the likelihood of viral infections diminishes. Buying certified, virus-free stock for planting is equally important.

Strawberries

Hybrids of *Fragaria* (fam. *Rosaceae*), derived from *F. chiloensis* and *F. virginiana*.

Hardy perennial herbaceous plant with a cropping life of about 3 years.

Size: 15-30 cm (6-12″) spread by 15-20 cm (6-8″) high.

Planting to harvesting time: 6-10 months.

Yield: from 115-450 g (4-16 oz) per plant.

With its mouth-watering red berries and distinctive aroma, the strawberry is perhaps the best loved of all summer fruits. Although their cultivation requires some care, strawberries are a very rewarding crop for the amateur; they are the quickest cropping of all fruits and summer varieties will give a good-sized harvest in their first year.

Unlike most other fruits, strawberries are produced on low-growing, herbaceous plants. The cropping life of the plants is short; strawberry beds are usually replanted with fresh stock after one to four seasons. However, most varieties readily reproduce themselves from runners; as long as your plants are healthy, you can propagate your own new stocks without any additional cost.

There are two main groups of garden strawberries, summer-fruiting varieties and perpetuals. **Summer fruiters** are by far the most popular, although they generally crop only once in the season. A few varieties may bear a second crop in the autumn if conditions are favourable.

Some of the new varieties produce exceptionally large fruit, weighing up to 90 g (3 oz) each, although many people consider the smaller berries to have a superior flavour.

Perpetual strawberries (or **remontants**) produce fruit all summer, beginning in mid-summer and continuing into autumn. Removing the first trusses of blossoms from the plants prevents overlapping with summer fruiting varieties and ensures a heavier yield from the later flushes. The berries are not as large as those of the summer fruiters, and they tend to produce fewer runners. There is one variety of perpetual strawberry which produces very long runners. It is known as the climbing strawberry. Strictly speaking it does not actually climb, but it can be trained and tied to trellises.

Although they are usually grown in beds, strawberries do very well in containers, such as barrels, window boxes, or special earthenware strawberry

A heavy crop of well grown strawberries is one of the home grower's finest rewards.

Harry Smith

pots. This obviously has great potential for a small garden, patio or balcony. The plants have very attractive leaves and flowers, and containers filled with strawberry plants make a delightful feature.

Strawberries are susceptible to a number of serious virus diseases. However, stocks have been improved by the introduction of government certification schemes. Buy disease-free certified stock if this is available. Summer and perpetual strawberries are not propagated from seed.

Suitable site and soil

Because strawberries bloom early in the year and the flowers are carried close to the ground, they are very susceptible to spring frosts. Frosted flowers turn black in the centre, and fail to fruit. The site must therefore be frost free, open and raised rather than low-lying. If your garden is on a slope, try to locate the strawberry bed towards the top, rather than the bottom, where frost and stagnant air would collect.

A sunny site is necessary for any successful strawberry growing, and early

1. Double dig the soil at least a month before planting, digging in plenty of manure or garden compost.

2. If plants are in peat pots, soak pots in water, then plant with rim of pot level with soil surface.

correctly planted   planted too high   planted too deep

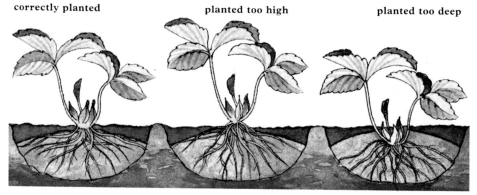

3. The crown of the plant must be just level with the soil. If planted too high, the roots may dry out; too deep, the crown may rot.

crops need shelter as well. If the site is too windy, pollinating insects will be less likely to visit the flowers.

Wild strawberries are found in rich woodland soil; cultivated strawberries are most successful if grown in a similar soil. It should be deep, with a high content of organic matter, and well drained. It must be moisture retentive as well, because crops are very dependant on a steady supply of water during the growing season.

A slightly acid soil, with a pH of 6.5 is best; if your soil is too limey, apply moist peat, garden compost or well-rotted manure. Light loams are preferable to very heavy soils, because they warm up more quickly in spring and give earlier crops. Diseases, such as redcore, are also more likely to develop on very heavy soils.

Do not make a strawberry bed on land which is newly dug from turf. There is likely to be a very high wireworm population in such soils, and wireworm can severely damage strawberry plants.

Because strawberry beds should be rotated every three or four years, many people find it most convenient to grow them as part of the vegetable garden. Remember, though, that strawberry plants should not follow potatoes, as they are subject to many of the same diseases.

Preparation and planting

Begin preparing the soil in early spring or mid-summer, at any rate at least a month before planting. If the site has been well prepared for previous vegetable crops, just fork it over lightly and check for weeds. Otherwise, double dig to encourage a good root run, but keep the topmost soil uppermost. Make sure you have removed all traces of perennial weeds. Besides making cultivation difficult, they harbour pests and diseases and a weedy strawberry bed will never crop well.

Dig in well-rotted manure or garden compost at the rate of half a garden barrow load per sq m (sq yd). This opens up a heavy soil and improves the moisture retaining capacity of a light one. If neither is available, work in moist peat or leafmould at the same rate and scatter and rake in an equal parts (by weight) mixture of hoof and horn fertilizer, sterilized bonemeal and sulphate of potash, at 180 g per sq m (6 oz per sq yd). After digging, lightly roll or tread down, and rake the surface smooth.

Plant summer fruiting strawberries in late summer, early autumn, or mid-spring. Plant perpetuals in late autumn, only when soil conditions are first class; otherwise wait until spring. You will not lose a crop by waiting.

Plant in crumbly, friable soil; wait if excessive rain has made the bed sticky, or if the soil is dry. Planting strawberries close together increases the yield from the plot as a whole, but reduces the yield per plant. Also, the size of the individual berries is likely to be reduced. A sensible compromise is to leave 45 cm (18″) between plants and 75 cm (2′6″) between rows, with 23 cm (9″) between plants of compact varieties. Leave slightly more space around plants you intend to use for propagation only, so the runners have room to fully develop.

It is important to plant strawberries at just the right depth. If you plant them too deeply, the crowns rot; if they are too shallow, the roots may dry out. The soil level should be midway up the crown.

Make a shallow hole with a small 5 cm (2″) mound in the centre, and set the plant on top of the mound. Spread the roots out over and down the mound to their full extent. If the plants come in peat pots, do not remove them but soak the pots in water for 10 minutes, and then plant at once with the rim of the pot just level with the soil surface. Always plant firmly, then water. Preferably, plant in the evening, but if this is not possible, shade the plants temporarily from strong sunshine.

Cultivation and care outdoors

Water frequently, possibly every day in the early weeks, especially if planted in summer, until the young plants are established. Then judicious watering is called for. Thereafter, unless there is a drought, you will probably not have to water them, once they are established, until the fruits are beginning to swell. Then water once, at the rate of 20 L per sq m (4½ gal per sq yd). This should suffice, unless the weather is very dry.

In late spring the plants will develop stolons, which are long runners with a plantlet at each joint. Cut these off at their point of origin, unless they are needed for propagation.

No feeding is needed as plants come quickly into bearing, but competing weeds should be kept down by light hoeing or hand weeding. If you have cleared the ground of all perennial weeds prior to planting, the only problem will be from annual weeds. The combination of weeding and mulching should be enough; avoid using chemical herbicides.

Removing all the blossom on summer fruiting varieties in their first spring gives more than two seasons' crop the following year, but few gardeners have the patience to wait that long. If planting was done after the beginning of autumn, however, it is essential to take off the first season's blossom. Perpetual varieties should always have their first season's blossom removed to allow them to build up strength for fruiting.

4. If planting after autumn, cut off first season's blossom, so plants build up strength for future crops.

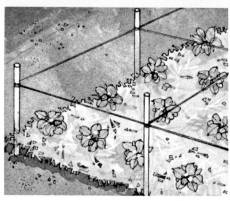

5. To protect crops from birds, make a frame for netting by stretching wires between vertical posts.

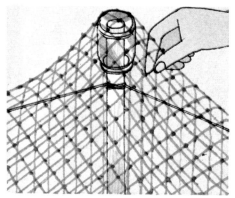

6. Invert jars over posts before putting on netting; this stops the netting from catching on the posts.

7. Water frequently and thoroughly until plants are established, particularly in hot, dry weather.

8. Hoe if necessary to keep weeds down, being careful not to damage roots. Avoid using chemical herbicides.

9. Control greenfly by spraying with derris or bioresmethrin according to manufacturers' instructions.

10. Protect ripening fruit with a layer of barley straw, special strawberry mats, or plastic strips.

11. Pick berries when they are firm and evenly coloured; snap off stem and avoid bruising ripe fruit.

Care of the fruit

To keep the ripening fruit off the ground and free from soil splashes, strawberry beds are traditionally covered with barley straw. Besides keeping the fruit clean, it acts as a mulch, conserving soil moisture. Wheat straw is harder to obtain and oat straw is more likely to carry pests. Try to obtain straw which has been properly thrashed, otherwise grains left in it will sprout. Do not spread the straw until the weight of the developing berries is pulling them down to the ground. Premature strawing cuts them off from ground warmth, increasing the risk of damage from late spring frosts. Spread the straw thickly but evenly round each plant, tucking it under the fruit.

Many gardeners will find it difficult to obtain straw nowadays. Buy special strawberry mats or use black plastic strips instead. Keep the plastic in place with a few stones and make sure that it slopes evenly away from the plants so that pools of water cannot collect around them. If slugs are likely to be a problem, scatter a few slug pellets around the plants before putting down the fruit protector.

Protect the crop from birds with either a permanent fruit cage or with light-weight plastic netting spread over the beds. Drive in short posts and run taut wires between them. These can remain in place for the life of the bed. Invert glass jars over the tops of the posts so that the netting will slide without catching. Protect the plants with netting when the berries begin to swell, because mice and squirrels take while they are still green. Make sure the netting clears the tops of the plants and can be removed easily for picking.

Early cropping

An extra early crop can be grown under cloches or plastic tunnels or in a greenhouse. An unheated greenhouse has no advantage over cloches, although a heated one will give crops from mid-spring. For the best results, hand-pollinate all forced strawberries to avoid mis-shapen unattractive fruits. Use a camel hair brush; dab the flowers daily when they have fully opened.

Outdoors, crops can be forwarded by three or four weeks using glass cloches, or by two or three weeks with plastic cloches or tunnels. Many varieties crop earlier than usual in their first year, so do protect your maiden plants. First year plants will also be smaller, so plant them 23 cm (9″) apart, allowing 90 cm (3′) between rows—the wider spacing makes the placing of cloches and tunnels easier. After the maiden crop has been picked, pull out alternate plants and leave the

1. Begin forcing under cloches in late winter; in warm weather, open cloches or space them slightly apart.

2. For strawberries grown under plastic tunnels, lift the fabric for spraying, pollinating and harvesting.

rest uncovered.

There is no point in using cloches or tunnels too early; the beginning of late winter is quite soon enough. Before covering, weed the bed and scatter slug pellets around the plants. There is no need to 'straw' the beds but the plants must be protected from birds with netting, while the cloches or tunnels are opened during the ripening period.

Using tunnels will lead to poor berry development unless insects are allowed to fly in to pollinate the blossom. Open the tunnel wide in the middle part of the day when the flowers are out. Most glass cloches have spaces through which insects can enter, but in very hot weather, open the cloches or space them 5 cm (2″) apart.

For greenhouse forcing, plant rooted runners singly in 15 cm (6″) pots filled with John Innes No. 3 potting compost, doing this in early summer if possible, and certainly by late summer. Keep the pots indoors until early in mid-winter, making sure that the plants have enough water and are not cracked by frost. Once inside the greenhouse, keep the plants quite cool with no artificial heat until signs of growth can be seen, usually ten days or two weeks later. Now supply heat to raise the temperature very gradually, reaching a maximum of 10 °C

(50°F) by the end of mid-winter. Increase humidity by damping down.

Once the flowers have set and the berries begun to swell, allow the temperature to rise still further, ideally to 18°C (65°F), and maintain moist conditions until the fruit starts to colour, when the air should again be drier. Feed the plants occasionally with dilute liquid manure or fertilizer as the berries swell. Forked sticks or bent galvanized wire can be used to hold the fruit trusses up. Forced plants cannot be used again.

Container growing

There are special pots for growing strawberries but you can make your own container by drilling 5–7 cm (2–3″) holes in the side of a barrel. Put a layer of hardcore in the bottom of the container. Barrels should have a central core of drainage material running up through the middle; make a wire mesh tube, 10–15 cm (4–6″) in diameter; place this in the middle of the container and fill it with clean hardcore. The tube should end 10 cm (4″) below the surface of the compost. Use John Innes No. 3 potting compost and work upwards, inserting the roots of the plants into the holes from the outside. Water as you proceed with the planting. Water growing plants regularly.

1. **Plunge small pots filled with compost into the soil close to the parent plant.**

2. **Peg down the runners either directly into the soil or into pots; fasten with wire hooks or hairpins.**

3. **Additional runners may form from the selected plantlet; cut these off as they drain the plant's vigour.**

4. **Once the plants have rooted, sever the runner from its parent plant with a sharp knife.**

Propagation

Strawberries are usually not much good for cropping after three or four years because virus infection has taken its toll by then. However, they are easily increased from runners. Before beginning to replace old stock from runners, make sure the parent plants are free of all pests and diseases, especially viruses. It is not worth propagating from diseased or infested plants.

For the best results, select healthy, one-year-old parent plants, and do not allow them to bear fruits. By removing the flowers, all the plant's energy is channelled into the production of first class runners. The runners should be ready for pegging down from mid-summer to late autumn. Although a healthy growing parent plant will produce numerous runners, select the strongest four or five, and allow only one plant to develop on each.

You can peg down the runners directly into the soil, if it has been lightly cultivated beforehand, or you can peg them into pots. Fill the pots with John Innes No. 1 potting compost and either sink them into the ground so their rims are level with the soil surface, or stand them firmly on the surface. Peg the runners down into the soil and fasten securely with wire hooks or stout hairpins. Once the runner has rooted, a further runner may form at the point of rooting; pinch this out.

About a month after pegging down, the young plants should be ready for moving. Check that the plant has made good leaf growth, which is a sure sign of successful rooting. Then cut the runners from the parent plant. If you are lifting the plants directly from the soil, use a trowel and make sure there is a good ball of soil around the roots. Whether they are open grown or pot grown, the new plants should be planted into their final positions immediately. If you do not want the young plants to crop in their first season, pick off the flowers as they form. An increased second year crop will result. The variety *Royal Sovereign* responds to this treatment well.

Harvesting

Strawberry plants usually crop for three or four weeks. However, in very hot seasons, harvesting may be over after a week or two. Perpetual strawberries carry much smaller crops at any one time, but may continue producing berries for several months.

As soon as the fruits are full sized, they will colour quickly. Pick them when the fruits are firm and evenly coloured all over. Because strawberries go mouldy very quickly, it is best to pick them when the weather is fine and the fruits dry. Pick over the bed daily during harvest time, to avoid over-ripe fruit. As you inspect the beds, remove any rotting or damaged fruit to avoid the spread of disease. Burn any infected fruit, do not leave it on the ground or put it on the compost heap.

Take the strawberries with the stalk intact. Always handle the berry by the stalk, so you do not bruise or discolour the flesh. You can remove the stalk and calyx just before serving. Strawberries for jam-making can be picked with or without the stalk. Use the fruits as quickly as possible, as strawberries do not remain at their best for long.

Aftercare

Late in the season, leaves begin to wither. If you leave the foliage on plants after harvesting, pests and diseases are more likely to be a problem with next year's crops. Cutting the old leaves exposes the crowns to light and air and renews their vigour. Some varieties, like *Talisman,* will crop again in autumn if the leaves are cut after the first harvest.

There are two methods of clearing strawberry beds: burning and mowing. The first is more drastic and more likely to go wrong, although it does kill off many pests. The safer method is cutting off the leaves, and raking them up along with the straw. Use a hand sickle, shears, or, for very long beds, a mower. Remember that the crowns must not be damaged, so if you do mow over the plants, set the cutter for 10 cm (4″). After mowing, clean the beds generally, removing stray runners and weeds. Do not put any of the rakings on the compost heap; burning them in a bonfire is better as it will cut down disease risk.

After the bed is completely cleaned, fork in sulphate of potash at the rate of 15 g per sq m (½ oz per sq yd). A light mulch put on at this time will also help to build up the crowns and keep the autumn crop of weeds from sprouting. Check your strawberry netting for holes, and do any repairs before you put it away.

Exhibition tips

Because strawberries can be so easily bruised, fruits for exhibition should be handled as little as possible, and picked just before the show. The usual number of strawberries exhibited is 20; use scissors to cut the fruits from the plant. Remember that strawberries can be damaged by their own weight, so when packing them for the show do not put too many in one container. Display the berries on a plate in neat rows, so they can be easily counted. The judge will look for large, ripe fruit with even colour and free from blemishes. The stalks, which should be fresh and green, must still be attached.

Varieties

Early
Cambridge Vigour: first-year plants crop early; older plants crop mid-season. Plant upright, large with vigorous foliage; fruit large, conical, orange-red turning to scarlet later; sweet flesh, fine flavour. Crops best in first year, after which crops diminish. Susceptible to wilt and botrytis, but resistant to redcore. Excellent for freezing; smaller late berries good for jam-making.

Cambridge Rival: tall, open, vigorous plant. Fruits dark crimson, conical shaped, large at first, becoming smaller; firm flesh, scarlet; excellent, sweet flavour. Susceptible to wilt, bruises easily.

Grandee: very large berries, up to 7.5 cm (3″) diameter, 90 g (3 oz) in weight. Heavy cropper, particularly in second year, up to 1.6 kg (3½ lb) per plant.

Gorella: well flavoured, large berries, dark red, wedge shaped.

Maincrop
Cambridge Favourite: reliable, heavy cropper; plant large, spreading; fruits large, pinky red, firm, pale pink flesh; moderate flavour, slightly pine tasting. Most common commercial variety; resistant to mildew, but prone to green petal. Crops well in open, under cloches and in frames, very long season.

Redgauntlet: plant medium large, spreading, vigorous; fruit very large, crimson red; round conical or wedge shaped; firm, dark scarlet flesh. Heavy cropper, but flavour only moderate; can be cropped again in autumn; very suitable for cooler, northern areas. Some resistance to mildew.

Aromel: berries medium red, good size and flavour; crops continually through to mid-autumn.

Royal Sovereign: plant very vigorous and leafy. Fruit medium to large, scarlet berries; sweet-flavoured, light red flesh. First class strawberry, but only moderate crops and is rather subject to fungal and viral infections.

Cambridge Aristocrat: rich flavour, reminiscent of alpine strawberry, long conical fruits; crops over long period.

Late
Cambridge Late Pine: vigorous, open plant; flowers less likely to be frosted; fruit medium to large size; rounded, very sweet, dark flesh; heavy cropper; partially mildew resistant.

Domanil: Belgian variety; berries medium to large; very heavy cropper.

Talisman: mid to late season; vigorous plant, upright dense growth, slow to start growth; fruit scarlet; large fruit getting smaller late in season; crops a second time in autumn; resistant to red core and mildew; needs good soil to do well and adequate moisture.

Perpetual (early summer to mid-autumn)
Hampshire Maid: very good late summer cropper; rounded, conical, large fruit; well flavoured; needs watering in dry weather; produces very few runners.

Gento: continental variety; good crops of very large, conical berries with slight acid flavour; crops heavily late summer to mid-autumn; also crops on runners as well as parent plant.

Sonjana: 'climbing' strawberry; fruits on long runners (as well as parent plant) which can be trained up trellises although runners do not actually climb on their own.

Redgauntlet

Pests & Diseases

Although the number of pests and diseases affecting strawberries is formidable, the amateur gardener is unlikely to meet more than one or two of them. Because many of the infections are not visible in the early stages, and healthy looking plants may in fact be diseased, it is extremely important to buy certified virus-free plants. Remember, though, this does not guarantee that the plants will remain disease-free permanently. It is up to you to keep your strawberry bed in good health.

Aphids: greenfly can infest strawberries from early spring onwards, feeding on the leaves, so that they are curled and twisted and the plants stunted. The main danger, however, is that they carry virus diseases which are incurable.

Watch the plants carefully for any indication of aphids, starting in early spring. If necessary, spray with derris or bioresmethrin.

Strawberry beetle: this is the most damaging beetle which attacks the strawberry. It is mostly black and about 1.3-2 cm ($\frac{1}{2}-\frac{3}{4}''$) long. It feeds on the flesh, leaving an open wound in the fruit, and sometimes removes the seeds. Because the beetle lives in rough grass, leaf litter or weeds, the best precaution is to make sure the area surrounding the strawberry bed is well cultivated and any grass is kept mown.

Red spider mite: these are not actually spiders, but tiny, pale red or orange mites which suck the sap from the leaves. The leaves then turn pale yellow or grey-brown, and the plant is generally weakened. Sometimes silken webs are visible on the leaves which are infested. Keep the plants well supplied with water as these pests thrive in hot, dry conditions, and spray with malathion as soon as any signs of spider mite appear.

Strawberry eelworm: these microscopic pests live in the buds, leaf axils and leaves of strawberry plants; the main symptoms of infestation are thickened leaf stalks, puckered leaves and generally stunted growth, but this trouble is difficult to diagnose and may need professional advice. Once the soil has been infested with eelworm, all the plants should be burned and no strawberries grown on that plot for three years. Because runners from infested plants may also carry eelworm, it is best not to propagate from diseased plants. As a further precaution against the spread of eelworm, apparently healthy runners for propagation grown in the same bed should be completely immersed in hot water (43°C, 110°F) for 20 minutes, before potting into sterilized compost.

Snails and slugs: damage from these pests is usually worse on wet, badly-drained soil, or in badly kept gardens full of debris and leaf litter. Rough holes in the leaves and berries, and silvery slime trails are the most usual symptoms. The best precaution is to keep your garden clean and freely drained; controls are either methiocarb pellets or containers of sweetened milk sunk in the soil.

Strawberry weevil: the adults of various types of weevil attack the stalks of the leaves, flowers and fruit, breaking them off, and may feed on the developing fruit itself. In a bad infestation which, however, seldom occurs, the crop can be severely damaged without this being realised until too late. If you see stems hanging limply on many plants, suspect weevils, remove and burn all the

Donald Smith

Pale yellow crinkled leaves with silken webs are symptoms of red spider mite infestations.

damaged parts, and spray or dust the plants and soil with derris.

Tarsonemid mite: these are most destructive in the south of England, during very warm weather. The minute, colourless insects overwinter in the plants and feed on the unfolding leaves which remain small and become brown with down-curled edges. The mites remain inside the folded leaves or low down in the crowns of the plants, and chemical controls available to the gardener are not very effective. Keeping the plants well watered helps; dusting with flowers of sulphur in spring and early summer gives some control.

Botrytis: sometimes called grey mould, this fungus is worse in wet weather, when it can quickly turn berries into rotten, furry fruits useless for eating. Some varieties are more susceptible than others: *Royal Sovereign*, *Cambridge Favourite* and *Talisman* are particularly vulnerable. It is spread both by spores carried on the wind and by contact with diseased fruit, and so healthy berries can quickly become diseased. Because many weeds are host plants for botrytis, a weed-free garden is less likely to be infected. Plants grown in cramped, badly ventilated conditions, whether in the open or under cloches, are also very vulnerable. Remove and burn any mouldy berries immediately, and, as a precaution, the plants can be sprayed with thiram or captan according to manufacturer's instructions, but not fruit which is to be preserved in any way.

Leaf spot: this fungal disease rarely causes any serious trouble. Tiny, dark red, circular spots appear on the leaves, late in the season. If the infection is severe, the spots join up and the whole leaf withers. Cutting off the foliage after harvesting is a good control, and spraying with Bordeaux mixture in mid-spring the following year, if the attack was bad, is a good preventive measure.

Strawberry mildew: the variety *Royal Sovereign* is most susceptible to strawberry mildew, which appears as dark blotches on the upper surfaces of the leaves, and grey patches beneath. Eventually, the leaf edges will curl upwards, and show the fungal growth beneath. Spray with dinocap just before the plants flower, and two or three times again, at fortnightly intervals.

Red core: this is a serious root disease affecting strawberries, and is most likely to occur on badly drained soils. The soil-borne fungus turns the roots of an infected plant black or brown on the outside, with a red core. Above ground symptoms are stunted plants with wilted leaves, later reddish or brown, and fruiting poorly. Usually only a few plants in a whole bed will be infected to start with; eventually more and more plants look as though they were suffering from drought, wilt suddenly and die. Unfortunately, there is no completely

Strawberry beetles feed on the fruits, and remove the seeds from the undersides.

Botrytis, or grey mould, can quickly turn berries into rotten furry, inedible fruits.

effective cure; affected plants should be lifted and destroyed, and the land left free of strawberries for at least 13 years. Some varieties, however, are more resistant than others, for instance *Talisman, Cambridge Vigour* and *Cambridge Rival. Royal Sovereign* is one of the most vulnerable varieties.

Verticillium wilt: if you are growing potatoes near your strawberry patch and they have verticillium wilt, it is likely your strawberries are also infected. This soil-borne fungal disease causes plants to wilt for no apparent reason; leaves turn brown and die, and any fruits are small and malformed. There is no complete cure, once infected, and plants are best burnt, but soaking with benomyl solution will give some control.

Yellow edge: this virus is spread by aphids; it is also called Little Leaf because the leaves of infected plants gradually become smaller and smaller. The young leaves of infected plants develop yellow edges. The symptoms are most noticeable in mid-spring or early autumn, less so in summer.

Crinkle: there are two forms of this viral infection: mild and severe. Mild crinkle shows as tiny spots on the leaves and may affect cropping slightly. Severe crinkle is much more serious; symptoms are numerous yellow spots on the leaves, which become crinkled and wrinkled.

Arabis mosaic virus: the symptoms of this virus, which is spread by eelworm, vary according to the variety of strawberry grown, but generally the leaves become blotched with yellow, and the plant's fruiting capacity is diminished. Try not to grow strawberries too near hedgerows, as eelworms are much more numerous in the soil near hedges.

Green petal: the symptoms of this disease can first be seen in spring; the leaves are small and curled upwards, and the flowers have green petals instead of white ones. Any fruits which form will be small, mis-shapen and very seedy. In late summer, infected plants will have grey-green leaves which wilt inexplicably; any leaves which form later will be small and yellow. Many garden weeds, particularly clover, are host plants for this virus. Leafhoppers transmit the disease from host plants to strawberries, especially in dry weather.

GUIDE TO STRAWBERRY TROUBLES

Symptoms	*Probable causes*
Stunted plants with curled, twisted leaves	Aphids
Holes in flesh, seeds removed from underside of berry	Beetle
Leaves pale yellow or grey brown, silk webs on leaves	Red spider mite
Stunted growth, thickened leaf stalks, puckered leaves	Strawberry eelworm
Holes in leaves and berries, silvery slime trails	Slugs
Leaves stunted, brown with down-curled edges	Tarsonemid mite
Fruits, leaves covered with grey, furry mould	Botrytis cinerea
Tiny dark red circular spots on leaves	Leaf spot
Dark blotches on upper surfaces; grey mould beneath	Strawberry mildew
Plants stunted with wilted leaves; roots black or brown on outside, with red core	Red core
Plants wilt for no apparent reason; fruits small and malformed	Verticillium wilt
Young leaves develop yellow edges, new leaves small	Yellow edge virus
Leaves have yellow spots, become crinkled and wrinkled	Crinkle
Leaves blotched with yellow	Arabis mosaic virus
Flowers have green petals, fruits misshapen and seedy	Green petal virus
Stalks of leaves, buds and fruit partially or completely severed	Strawberry weevils